Famous Legends

This edition published 2022
by Living Book Press
Copyright © Living Book Press, 2022

ISBN: 9781234567890 (hardcover)
        9781234567891 (softcover)

First published in 1904.

This edition is based on the 1904 printing by The Century Co.

All rights reserved. No part of this publication may be reproduced, stored in a retrieval system, or transmitted in any other form or means – electronic, mechanical, photocopying, recording or otherwise, without the prior permission of the copyright owner and the publisher or as provided by Australian law.

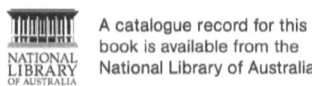

A catalogue record for this book is available from the National Library of Australia

Famous Legends

by

EMELINE G. CROMMELIN

adapted and edited by
LISA KELLY

A NOTE FROM THE PUBLISHER

This edition was produced in conjunction with Lisa Kelly, the educator behind A Mind in the Light, a Charlotte Mason curriculum.

Here's a few words from Lisa—

"As an educator and a mother of two lovely daughters, I spent a great deal of time searching for a curriculum which matched the ardent hope in my heart to nurture the minds of my children as well as their hearts.

Over time I found that the ideas and methods of Charlotte Mason came the nearest to matching the educational principles I could embrace. I added some ideas from Classical methods, but mostly I tried to shine a light on the hidden principles within Charlotte Mason's own books and her PNEU programs. From this was born my own curriculum: A Mind in the Light.

This curriculum reflects the depth of my feelings for each and every child's mind and endeavors to give teachers the tools they need to create an atmosphere of learning which stretches, delights and inspires, leading a student to the light. In this light, the mind finds truth, beauty and good."

Learn more about A Mind in the Light at
https://www.amindinthelight.com/

Contents

Robin Hood	5
King Arthur	26
Roland	39
St. Denis	51
The Cid	55
The Unknown Island	63
Brian Boru	73
The Monk and the Bird's Song	79
Sigurd	83
Frithiof	91
William Tell	109
The Bell of Atri	116
King Robert of Sicily	119
The Pied Piper of Hamelin	123
The Emperor's Sleep	129
The Lorelei	132
Index of Proper Names	135

"The strange and antiquated rhymes
With melodies of olden times;
As over some half-ruined wall,
Disjointed and about to fall,
Fresh woodbines climb and interlace.
And keep the loosened stones in place."
~LONGFELLOW— *Tales of a Wayside Inn.*

INTRODUCTION

This little book of famous legends needs no introduction beyond a word of emphasis as to its educational value.

It is needless to point out, perhaps, that these stories— handed down from father to son and circulated in minstrelsy before the days of written history— have been almost the sole preservatives of the romance, chivalry, and splendor of the Middle Ages.

Out of the wealth of myths and traditions my selections have been purposely diverse, that as far as possible each nation and each people might be represented in this marshaling of the picturesque in legendary history.

And thus may the young reader have an insight into what, in the case of each nation, has become of the very fiber of its literature, art, and music.

In some cases, where the beauty depends largely on the literary style and treatment, direct transcripts from the best sources have been made; but for the most part I have reduced the stories to the simplest terms consistent with clearness and human interest. Among the sources drawn upon are Guerber's *Legends of the Middle Ages* and *Myths of Northern Lands*, Chenoweth's *Stories of the Saints*, Washington Irving's "The Phantom Island", Baldwin's "The Story of Roland", Browning's poems, Longfellow's poems, Malory's *Boys' King Arthur*, Ragozin's "Frithjof" and "Roland", etc.

It is the author's hope and belief that this volume will help to inculcate in the child a love for good reading, quicken his imagination, and broaden his horizon.

EMELINE G. CROMMELIN. FEBRUARY 10TH, 1904

Robin Hood

   .   .   .   I think there is not one.
But he of Robin Hood hath heard and Little John,
And to the end of time the tales shall ne'er be done
Of Scarlock, George a Green, and Much the Miller's son,
Of Tuck, the merry friar, which many a sermon made
In praise of Robin Hood, his outlaws and their trade.
           ~Drayton.

Even the wild outlaw, in his forest-walk,
Keeps yet some touch of discipline.
        ~Old Play.

I. IN SHERWOOD FOREST

It was when Richard I, called the Lion-hearted, was king of England that Robin Hood and his merry men lived in Sherwood Forest.

Some people say that when Robin Hood was young he recklessly spent the money he had inherited; and, being an adventurous youth, he fled to the forest that ever since has been associated with his name.

Whether Robin was forced to live there or not, he loved its freedom and wild beauty better than anything else in the world. He loved its thickly wooded hills and valleys, its sparkling streams, and its carpet of bright green; its flowers of every color, and the songs of its birds. Robin was a mere lad when he first made the forest his home. As he grew older, one after another joined him, until he had more than a hundred men, who not only obeyed him, but loved him as well. It was not long before Robin Hood was looked upon as a kind of king, and he and his men defied the laws that the real kings made. They spent much of their time in stopping travelers on their way, and robbing them, or killing the king's deer, with which Sherwood Forest abounded.

It was on this game that the poor Saxons had lived when they were driven into the forest and hemmed in by their enemies. The Normans, who ruled the land, made such severe laws that it was dangerous to hunt or kill the deer, which had been a common dish for the Saxons before they were conquered.

Now Robin Hood was not altogether bad, for he did

A Statue of Richard Coeur de Lion

many things that were to his credit. He always spared the poor and the weak, never allowed a woman to be oppressed, and divided all booty with his men.

II. MAID MARIAN

IF you have heard of Robin Hood, you have heard also of Maid Marian, the fair Saxon maid, whom everyone loved. She, too, loved the beauty and freedom of the wild woods—the birds, the flowers, and the streams. It was amid such scenes that she had lived, from the time she was a child. She had learned from her mother how to dress wounds, and she knew a great deal about the herbs in the forest which had been her school.

Maid Marian was often mistress of the sports in her woodland home. Indeed, she handled the bow with such skill that she could shoot a running deer or flying bird, and thought it no uncommon feat. Robin and Marian met often in their beloved Sherwood Forest. Often they took long walks together, when the hunt was over. Often they sat beneath the old oaks that met above their heads. Often Robin sang some old Saxon song to the notes of Marian's harp. Thus it was that, amid the beauty and the music of the grand old forest, the youth and the maiden grew to love each other. And when deep sorrow came to Marian, no one spoke such gentle words of comfort as Robin.

Marian and her father had not joined in any of the merry times among the hunters since her mother's death, until the day that was the beginning of a new grief. Their friends welcomed them with great joy, and Marian's father, who was a minstrel, was asked to sing for the company. Taking the harp from his daughter, the minstrel began an old Saxon war song, in which he told how the Saxons once owned the beautiful land, and hunted the deer in the vast forest as much as they pleased, till the Normans came and drove them from their cities, and made severe laws for those who lingered near their old homes; and how their unrelenting conquerors still wrought hardships upon them by killing the beasts and birds that filled the forest.

The song closed with words of sorrow for the friends who had been taken away and would never return.

It was in this fashion that the wandering minstrels used to chronicle in song the mighty deeds of friend and foe. Had it not been for them, many of our most delightful stories, which were remembered from father to son, would have been lost. When people knew how to write these tales, the old minstrels were needed no longer.

> The last of all the bards was he,
> Who sung of Border chivalry;
> For, well-a-day their date was fled,
> His tuneful brethren all were dead;
> And he, neglected and oppress'd,
> Wished to be with them, and at rest.
>
> A wandering harper, scorn'd and poor,
> He begged his bread from door to door,
> And tuned, to please a peasant's ear,
> The harp a king had loved to hear.
> ~SIR WALTER SCOTT - *Lay of the Last Minstrel.*

Just as Marian's father finished the last words of his song, an arrow came whizzing through the air, and struck the harp. This was the beginning of an attack by the foresters, in which Marian's father was killed.

It was not long after this that Robin's father was slain by one of the foresters, and Robin declared he would have revenge. He knew to whom the arrow belonged, for it was marked with a crown between the feathers. Taking it in his hand, he said: "I shall never rest until I have found the owner of this arrow, and avenged my father's death." His mother, who was overcome by the loss of her husband, soon followed him, and Marian and Robin were both without father or mother.

III. ROBIN HOOD MADE LEADER

The king had heard so much about Robin Hood killing his deer and defying his foresters, that he sent the sheriff to capture the bold outlaw without delay. But Robin was too much for the sheriff, who lost his life by a well-aimed arrow from Robin's bow. After this sheriff was buried, a man whom Robin had caught and bound in the forest was appointed in his place.

The condition of the poor Saxons seemed to grow ever worse; and Robin was anxious to find out for himself just how affairs stood. So he disguised himself as a beggar, and went to a part of the forest where the Saxons were cutting wood for the abbeys.

Robin Hood

He begged the men to give him something to do. They told him to go to the sheriff, if he would feed himself and a Norman.

"Bad times these are, indeed," said Robin, "when a Saxon works that a Norman may eat and play."

"Yes," answered one of the wood-cutters, "but there are worse times coming."

Many encounters between the oppressors and the oppressed followed. Finally, Robin Hood, who had been so successful in fighting the enemy, was looked upon as a powerful leader among the Saxons. They hoped he would be able to free them from the rule of the Normans. At last a number of them held a meeting, and decided to build a house in a secluded part of the forest. The house was to be well protected, and surrounded by a moat, or ditch filled with water, and to be entered by ladders only.

Then Robin Hood was chosen leader of the band, because he was the most skillful with his bow, and the most popular with the people.

The men promised, on Robin's bow, to be true to him and to one another; to obey all his orders, and keep secret all he told them.

Then Robin made them promise never to rob the poor nor trouble the weak, but to help them if need be; never to strike a Saxon, unless struck first by him; never to harm women or children; and, last of all, to keep only what they needed of the booty, and to give the rest to the poor and needy.

It will be interesting to know how one after another

joined this little band in the forest, whose names were associated with their famous leader ever after.

IV. ALAN DALE

ONCE, when Robin and Marian were walking through the forest, they found a young harper, who seemed to be in great trouble. He told them his name was Alan Dale, and he was unhappy on account of a Saxon maid, whom he loved, and could not wed because he was poor. Her father and mother were trying to make her marry a rich Norman lord, whom she did not like.

Ellen, for that was the young girl's name, was kept at home with her parents, while Alan roamed through the forest, and sang sorrowful songs to the notes of his harp. When Robin and Marian had heard the sad story, they were determined to help the young couple.

It happened there was a fair in the dale, and Marian, dressed as a harper, attended it. She sang some old Saxon songs that Alan used to sing, and Ellen, listening, wondered and drew near.

Ellen was so near the harper that she was able to hear what Marian had come to tell her. It was soon arranged that Marian should remain with Ellen in her home, and teach her to play the harp, of which she was very fond.

When Robin came to Marian's home, and found she had not returned from the fair, he dressed himself as a beggar and came to Ellen's house to see if all were well.

He was able to see Marian, who whispered hurriedly to him at the door: "All is going well. I will stay here until the time for the wedding, when we will meet you at the church."

Then the beggar left the house, and no one except Marian knew that he was the bold Robin Hood of Sherwood Forest.

Of course Ellen was very happy that, when the time came for the wedding, Alan Dale was the bridegroom instead of the rich old lord, and Ellen was taken to live in the greenwood instead of the castle.

And there was another wedding that day, for Robin and Marian were married also. When Robin Hood's name was read out in church the people were surprised and startled. Then cheers were given for the bold outlaw and his band, as the happy couple went to their forest home.

A great feast had been prepared for them. The minstrel played and sang, and all made merry.

V. LITTLE JOHN

LITTLE John was second to Robin Hood in command. His real name was John Little, some people said; but he was called Little John because he was so tall, being over seven feet high.

One day, Robin went hunting with his men; but, finding the sport poor, he thought he would try it alone, and said:

"If I am in danger and cannot escape, I will blow my horn that you may come and help me."

He had not gone far when he came to a stream at the

foot of a hill. In the middle of the bridge over it, which was a single tree lying across the stream, he met a monstrous big man, and neither would let the other pass. After some angry words, Robin said:

"Let us fight this matter out on the bridge. The one who is able to push the other into the water shall be the victor."

The stranger agreed to this, and the matter was settled very quickly. They fought with great fury, and neither would give in. Finally, the stranger succeeded in throwing poor Robin into the water, and exclaimed:

"Where are you now, my good fellow?"

"Our battle is ended," cried Robin, as he waded to the bank of the stream, "and you are the victor."

Then Robin, who was wet to the skin, blew a loud blast on his horn. At once there appeared fifty of his men, all dressed in Lincoln green, who wanted to know what had befallen their leader.

Robin explained to them that the stranger had tumbled him into the water. At these words, the men were going to seize the stranger, who was quite ready and willing to fight them all; but Robin stopped them, saying:

"My friend, no harm shall come to you. These are my men, and, if you like, you shall be one of them. Will you join our band?"

"I will, with all my heart," answered the stranger, whose strength and courage had pleased Robin greatly.

When he told them his name, one of the number said he should be called Little John, by which name he was known ever after.

VI. FRIAR TUCK

A day of merrymaking had been appointed by Robin Hood and his men. There were jumping, racing, and shooting matches, for which prizes were given. The jugglers did wonderful tricks, and the minstrels sang and played. The holiday closed with a dance in the woodland by the hunters and their friends.

While one of these tests of strength and skill was being made, a member of the band told of a certain friar who could draw a bow with the greatest strength that ever he had seen.

As soon as Robin heard this, he made up his mind to see the famous friar, and started out with one of his men to find him. They had not gone far when Robin saw in the distance the friar walking by the water. He alighted from his horse, and called loudly:

"Carry me over the water, Friar, or you lose your life."

The friar said not a word; but did as he was told, and put Robin down on the other side of the stream. Just as he did so, however, he said to Robin:

"It is your turn now to carry me over the water, my bold fellow. You do so, or I shall make you sorry."

Robin looked surprised, but said not a word. Taking the friar on his back, he carried him across the stream, and put him down on the other side. Then he spoke to the friar as he had at first, when he told him to carry him over the water or he would lose his life.

The good-natured friar smiled, and took Robin on his shoulders, as before, but said not a word. When he reached the middle of the stream, however, he shook him off, and cried:

"Choose now for yourself whether you sink or swim."

Robin reached the shore after a good ducking, and began shooting arrows at the friar, who swam to a tree nearby. But Robin's arrows did not hurt the friar, who called:

"You may shoot at me all day, my bold fellow, and I shall stand it."

Robin did not mind these words, but kept on shooting until he had not one arrow left in his quiver. Then he and the friar fought with their swords, but neither would yield. At last, Robin asked the friar to hold his hand, and let him blow his horn. The friar consented. When the horn had sounded three times, behold, there appeared fifty men, all dressed in Lincoln green!

The astonished friar asked Robin who they were.

"They are my men," said Robin; " but that is nothing to you."

Then the friar, remembering that Robin blew his horn three times, asked that he might be allowed to whistle three times.

Robin consented with all his heart.

At once there appeared fifty-three raging dogs, who flew at Robin and his men. Then the friar cried to Robin:

"For every man there is a dog, and two for you."

Before Robin could believe what had happened, two dogs sprang upon his back, and tore his coat to bits. Then Little John and the others beat the dogs back. The friar, seeing he could not fight so many brave men even with his dogs, made an agreement with Robin Hood that he would live with him and be his chaplain. So the friar left his home in the dale, where he had lived seven years, and was known as Friar Tuck of Robin Hood's band.

VII. THE BARON

A number of the king's men, with a baron at their head, started out to capture Robin Hood. As they journeyed through the forest, they found a man bound to a tree, who seemed to be in great distress.

He was dressed as a beggar, and had been hurt in some way, they thought. The baron ordered his men to set the poor man free. The beggar thanked him graciously, and said:

"As I was coming through the forest, some robbers came up to me, and searched me for gold. Finding none, they tied me to this tree, where I have been ever since."

"They must have been Robin Hood's men," cried the baron.

To this the beggar nodded his head, and said: "They were divided into three bands, and were on their way to meet the men sent to capture them. They intended to kill the leader and to tie the others to trees and leave them to die."

The baron and his men were terrified, and seemed less eager to find Robin Hood and his men.

They thought they would have a good dinner before they continued the search. No sooner had the meat and bread been laid on the grass, and they were about to begin, when they heard the sound of a horn echo loudly through the forest. They stopped for nothing, but started to run as fast as they could.

In the meantime, the beggar whom they had set free was calling out Robin Hood's name. At once there appeared three bands of men, all dressed in Lincoln green, and carrying bows and short swords.

While the leaders and the bands were seizing the baron and his men, the beggar dropped his disguise, and appeared all dressed in Lincoln green, like Robin Hood's men— indeed, it was Robin Hood himself who had played this trick on the baron.

The baron, who held a written order to capture Robin Hood, and all his men were seized and guarded carefully. The dinner which they had prepared was eaten and enjoyed by the bold outlaw and his archers.

When they had finished, they invited the poor prisoners to eat also; but fear had taken away their hunger.

But Robin Hood did not treat them badly, after all. He took them to another part of the forest, and welcomed them to a fine feast, which they enjoyed. He made them promise never to take part in any attempt to capture Robin Hood or his men; never to refuse them shelter or help if they needed it; and that the baron should pay a sum of money every year for the support of Robin Hood and his men. Then he set them all free.

VIII. THE BISHOP

When Robin Hood heard that the bishop was coming, he and some of his men dressed themselves as shepherds, and waited in the forest for him and his company to pass. While they were waiting, they roasted a fine buck for dinner. As the bishop drew near, he noticed the delicious meat roasting, and, being very hungry, said to his followers:

"I believe those forest rovers, who are always giving trouble, are roasting some fine venison for dinner. If so, we shall eat it, and take the hungry prisoners to the king."

When the bishop reached the place, he asked one of the "shepherds" what he meant by roasting the king's venison, and told him it was the last time he would have a chance to do it.

The "shepherd" paid no heed to the bishop's words, but invited him to join them in their merry feast. The bishop became very angry at this, and ordered his men to bind the saucy fellow to a tree, and said they should all be taken to the king without delay.

Before the men had time to carry out the order, however, Robin blew a loud blast on his horn. In an instant the frightened bishop and his company were surrounded by a band of men, all dressed in Lincoln green, and carrying bows and short swords.

At the same time Robin Hood and the men who were with him dropped the dress of shepherds. There they stood, all dressed in Lincoln green, like the others who had come out of the forest so suddenly.

Now it was Robin's turn. He ordered Little John to bind the poor bishop, who cried: "Mercy, mercy, I pray! If I had known you, I should not have come this way."

Robin and his men went into the forest for a short distance, and ate their dinner. Then Little John spread the bishop's cloak on the ground, and on it emptied the bishop's bag of three hundred pounds. The bishop gave up the gold very willingly, because his life was saved.

But Robin did not intend to let him off so easily, so he asked Alan to bring his harp and play for the bishop to dance. Alan did so, and the bishop danced, in spite of his heavy riding-boots, until he fell exhausted to the ground. Then Robin bade the harper stop his music, and the worn-out bishop cried:

"You may shoot all the deer you wish in Sherwood Forest, and if you or any of your band ever catch me again you may hang me."

IX. KING RICHARD

KING Richard I had heard a great deal of Robin Hood's deeds and pranks. He wished to see the bold outlaw and his merry men, who roved as they liked through the forest. So the king and his twelve lords dressed themselves as friars, and rode to the place where they thought they would find Robin and his men.

When Robin saw the company of friars draw near, he mistook the king for the abbot, as he was taller than the others. He seized his horse by the head, and cried:

"It is against such fellows as you that I make war."

"We are messengers from the king," said the king himself; "and he is waiting, at a short distance from here, to speak to you."

"God save the king!" shouted Robin, "and all who wish him well."

"You are a traitor," cried King Richard, "for you do not wish him well yourself."

"If you were not one of his messengers," said Robin, "I should make you sorry for what you say. I am as true to the king as any of his subjects. I have never harmed any but those who live by taking from others that which does not belong to them. Come with me, for you are welcome—

> "All hail the lordlings of high degree,
>   Who live not more happy though greater than we.
> Our pastimes to see,
> Under every green tree.
>   In all the gay woodland, right welcome ye be."
>   ~MACDONALD

King Richard and his men wondered what sort of cheer Robin intended to give them; but they did not wonder long. Robin led the king's horse to his own tent, saying as he did so:

"I treat you this way because you come from the king. For his sake, no matter how much gold you may have with you, it is safe."

Then he blew a loud blast on his horn, and lo! from all directions came Robin Hood's men, all dressed in Lincoln green. There were a hundred and ten men, and every man bent the knee to Robin Hood.

The king was surprised to see them pay such respect to their master, and thought his courtiers might learn something from these woodland rovers. Then a fine dinner was prepared for the king and his lords, and they declared they had never dined better. Marian and Ellen were presented to the guests. When the feast was over, Robin and his archers entertained the company with such skillful archery as the king had never seen in any land before. He said to Robin, with whom he was greatly pleased:

"If I should get a pardon from King Richard, would you serve him well in all things?"

"With all my heart," answered Robin; and so said all his men with one accord.

Then, to the surprise of all the forest rovers and their bold leader, the king cried:

"It is King Richard who stands before you!"

At these words, Robin Hood and all his band fell on their knees before him.

But King Richard bade them rise, and told them he would give them the pardon he had promised, and that they should enter his service. He would make them his bodyguard, and they should remain in the castle with him as long as they desired.

When King Richard left the forest, Robin Hood rode by his side, and Marian and Ellen were in the gay procession. Never was there a grander display than when the king and his followers entered the city. They were welcomed by shouts and cheers from the crowd, rich and poor, young and old. When the people saw Robin Hood riding by the king's side, they cheered him also loudly.

And they are gone to London court,
  Robin Hood and all his train;
He once was there a noble peer,
  And now he's there again.

X. DEATH OF ROBIN HOOD

Robin Hood stayed at the castle until King Richard died. Then he and the faithful followers who had remained with him went back to the forest. They were glad to return to the freedom and the sports of the outdoor life, for which they had longed ever since they went with the king to his castle.

During the years that followed, Robin lost many of his men, which grieved him greatly. But a greater sorrow than all came when Marian was taken away. Just before she died, she reminded Robin, who stood beside her, of the happy days they had spent together in the forest.

Robin was never quite the same after Marian and some of his comrades had left him.

But when the new king offered a reward for his capture, he played some of his old tricks, and ruled in his forest home as long as he lived.

One day, poor Robin was wounded sorely in a fight. As he fled with all the strength he had left, he said to Little John, his faithful companion:

"I can shoot no more, for the arrows will not so fly. I am wounded. I will go to my cousin, the abbess, who lives near, and she may make me well again."

Robin reached Kirkley Hall, where his cousin dwelt. When he knew he could not live long with his failing strength, he blew three blasts on his horn. Little John, who sat under a tree nearby in the greenwood, heard the feeble sound, and said:

"Robin must be dying, for his blast is very weak."

When Little John reached him, Robin asked for his bow and arrows. Then, fitting an arrow into the bow carefully but slowly, he shot it from the window of Kirkley Hall, and said piteously:

"Bury me where the arrow falls, and place my bow at my side."

Little John did as his master wished, and Robin Hood was buried under the yew-tree, just where the arrow had fallen.

KING ARTHUR

...No man knew from whence he came,
But after tempest, when the long wave broke
All down the thundering shores of Bude and Bos,
There came a day as still as Heaven, and then
They found a naked child upon the sands
Of dark Tintagil by the Cornish sea;
And that was Arthur; and they fostered him;
Till he by miracle was approven king;
And that his grave should be a mystery
From all men like his birth.
~TENNYSON —*Idylls of the King: Guinevere*

ARTHUR MADE KING

Arthur was a famous king of England. He lived such a long time ago that we know, really, very little about him. This king had such strange adventures, and did such wonderful things, that people have never tired of writing and reading about him and his famous Knights of the Round Table.

It was not until Arthur had grown to young manhood, that he knew he was of royal blood. When this little prince was born, his father, King Uther, bade his attendants take the child, wrapped in cloth of gold, and give him to any poor man they met at the castle gate. It happened that the babe was given to Merlin, who was supposed to know all things.

Merlin took him to Sir Ector, who brought the child up as his own son, and Sir Ector's wife cared for him, and they called him Arthur.

When King Uther died, every lord in England wanted to be king. The wise Merlin had promised that it should be made known to them, by a wonderful sign, who should be king.

He called, therefore, all the lords together in a great church in London, on Christmas morning, to see if the sign would be given.

After the first prayers were said, there was discovered in the churchyard a great stone having four sides, with an anvil of steel in the middle of it, in which was a sword. About the sword, written in letters of gold, were these words:

"Whoso pulleth out this sword of this stone and anvil, is rightwise King born of England"

The lords went out to behold the stone and the sword. As soon as they saw the words that were written about the sword, they tried to move it; but it would not be stirred. "It will be made known to us," said the archbishop. So it was decided that ten famous knights should guard the sword until one came who should be able to move it.

On New Year's Day there was a great contest, when it was hoped it would be revealed to them who should be made king. All the barons came forth to the contest to try their skill. Among them rode Sir Ector, and with him his son, Sir Kay, and his foster- son, young Arthur.

But Sir Kay had no sword with him, having left his at his father's castle. He therefore asked Arthur to ride for his sword and bring it to him.

"I will, indeed," said Arthur, and rode as fast as he could; but when he reached the castle there was no one there to give him his brother's sword, for all had gone to the contest.

Then Arthur, being angry, said to himself: "I will ride to the churchyard, and take the sword from within the stone, for my brother, Sir Kay, shall not be without a sword this day."

When Arthur came to the churchyard, there was no one there. All the knights had gone to the contest to try their skill. Then Arthur, quickly and easily, pulled the sword out of the stone, and rode away to give it to his brother. As soon as Sir Kay saw it, he knew it was the sword of the stone, and went to his father, Sir Ector, and cried:

"Sir, here is the sword of the stone that appeared in the churchyard. It must be that I am chosen King of England."

When Sir Ector looked at the sword, he rode again to

the churchyard, with Sir Kay and Arthur, where he made Sir Kay swear how he came by the sword.

"Sir," said Sir Kay, "my brother, Arthur, brought it to me."

"And how came you by it?" asked Sir Ector of Arthur.

Then Arthur told how he had ridden to the castle for his brother's sword, and found no one there to give it to him. Knowing that Sir Kay should have a sword, he rode to the churchyard where he had seen the sword, and pulled it out of the stone easily.

"Were there no knights about the sword?" asked Sir Ector.

"No," answered Arthur.

"Then," exclaimed Sir Ector to Arthur, "I know now that you are chosen King of England."

"Wherefore should I be king?" asked Arthur.

"Sir," said Sir Ector, "because of the prediction that no man, save he that should draw out this sword shall be king of this land."

Then Sir Ector bade Arthur put the sword as it was before, that he might see for himself. So Arthur put the sword in the stone easily. Then did Sir Ector try to pull it out, but he could not move it.

"Now shall you try," said Sir Kay to Arthur.

"I will, indeed," said Arthur; and he pulled the sword out as easily as he had done before.

Then Sir Ector and Sir Kay both knelt on the ground before him.

"My father and my brother!" cried Arthur. "Why should you kneel to me?"

"No, no, I am not your father," exclaimed Sir Ector, "nor

am I even of your blood, which I now know is higher than I thought."

Then Sir Ector told Arthur how he was brought to him, soon after he was born, and had been to him like his own son.

Then was Arthur grieved when he knew that Sir Ector, who had cared for him, was not his father; that Sir Ector's wife, who had nourished him, was not his mother.

Arthur promised Sir Ector that if ever he (Arthur) should become king, he would never fail to do whatever Sir Ector might ask of him. Then was the archbishop told how the sword had been won, and by whom. But as this was not enough, all the barons came again on the twelfth day to try again who should be king. Still no one could move the sword, save Arthur only. This vexed the barons, who declared the kingdom should not be ruled by a boy who was not of royal blood. Again the contest was put off until another feast-day, when all the lords should meet. And when they met again, none could move the sword, as before, save Arthur only, who pulled it out easily. This grieved the barons so that it was put off until Easter. As Arthur had done before, so did he again at Easter. Still some of the lords were angry, and it was put off until another feast-day.

Then all manner of men tried to pull the sword from the stone; but none could move it, save Arthur only. He pulled it out easily before them all. Then the people cried:

"We will have Arthur for our king! Let there be no more delay. We see now that he is rightly chosen, and if any one holdeth against it, he shall not live."

Then all the people, both rich and poor, knelt before Arthur, and asked mercy because they had kept him waiting so long a time. The noble Arthur forgave them, and taking the sword that he had won, offered it upon the altar, and was made a knight. There it was he promised to be a true king as long as he should live.

King Arthur righted many wrongs that had been done since his father's death. The lands that had been taken from lords, knights, and ladies he caused to be returned to them, and he ruled the kingdom well.

THE SWORD EXCALIBUR

ONCE, when King Arthur and Merlin were riding through the forest, they came to a beautiful lake. In the middle of the lake the king saw an arm, clothed in white samite (a rich silken fabric), that held a fair sword in the hand.

"Look!" said Merlin; "that is the sword of which I told."

As Merlin spoke there appeared a damsel coming toward them on the lake. "That is the Lady of the Lake," said Merlin; "and if she comes to you, speak to her, and do whatsoever she asks of you."

"Fair damsel, what sword is that which the arm holds above the water yonder? I wish it were mine, for I broke my sword but now, in a fierce battle with a knight in the forest, and so I have none."

"Sir King," said the damsel, "that sword is mine. If you will give me whatever I shall ask, you shall have it."

"By my faith," said Arthur, "I promise you any gift you will ask of me."

Then the damsel, pointing to a barge on the lake, bade King Arthur row himself to the sword, and take it, with the scabbard. Then would she ask her gift of him, when she saw her time.

So the king and Merlin tied their horses, and rowed themselves to the sword that the hand held. King Arthur took it by the hilt, and the hand disappeared beneath the water.

Then they departed, and King Arthur liked his sword well.

There came into King Arthur's court, one day, a richly dressed lady. It was the Lady of the Lake. After she had saluted the king, she demanded of him the gift he had promised when she gave him the sword.

"True, indeed," said King Arthur; "but the name of the sword that you gave me I have forgotten."

"It is named," said the lady, "Excalibur."

"It is well," said King Arthur. "Ask what you will, and you shall have it, if I have the power to give it."

"I ask," said the lady, "the head of the knight that has won this sword, or else the head of the damsel who brought it."

"It cannot be," said King Arthur. "I may not grant you either of their heads, so ask what you will else, and it shall be granted."

"Then I shall ask nothing else of you," said the lady.

A poor knight, as he was departing from court, saw the Lady of the Lake. When he was told that she had demanded the head of King Arthur, he took his sword, and in the presence of the king smote off her head.

King Arthur was sorely grieved, and cried:

"Why have you done so? You have shamed me and all my court. This was the lady that gave me my sword, Excalibur, and she came hither under my protection. I shall never forgive you for this deed."

Then was there great sorrow in the court for the death of the Lady of the Lake, and King Arthur had her richly buried.

GUINEVERE MADE QUEEN

King Arthur told Merlin that his barons would give him no rest until he should take a wife, and asked his advice.

"It is well," said Merlin, "that you take a wife. Is there not one fair lady whom you love more than another?"

"Yes," answered King Arthur, "I love Guinevere, the daughter of King Leodogran, who holds in his house the famous Round Table. You told me that my father gave it to him."

So Merlin came to King Leodogran, and told him that King Arthur desired his daughter, the fair Guinevere, for his wife.

"These are good tidings to me," said King Leodogran, "that so noble and powerful a king as he should wish to wed my only daughter. I shall send him a gift also that will please him more than lands, for of lands he has enough. I shall give him the Round Table, which his father, King Uther, gave to me. When it is complete, there are a hundred and fifty knights. The hundred I have; but the fifty I lack, since so many have been slain during my time."

So the king gave his daughter, Guinevere, to Merlin to conduct her to King Arthur for his wife, and also the Round Table, with its hundred famous knights.

When King Arthur heard that Guinevere was coming, he rejoiced, for he had loved her long. He was more pleased with the gift of the Round Table and the hundred knights than he would have been with great riches.

The marriage of King Arthur and Guinevere was celebrated with great festivities. The Knights of the Round Table, who were the most powerful and the most worthy in all the land, were blessed in their seats. In every seat was the name, in letters of gold, of the knight who sat there.

King Arthur loved Queen Guinevere, and for her he did many splendid deeds.

DEATH OF KING ARTHUR

IT happened that while King Arthur was away from England, Sir Modred thought to rule in his stead. He sent letters, therefore, as if they had come from across the sea, telling that King Arthur had been slain in battle with one of his knights.

When King Arthur returned to his kingdom, there was a day set when he might be revenged on Sir Modred for this wrong.

Never was there seen a more sorrowful battle in all the land. King Arthur and Sir Modred stood between their hosts. They fought fiercely until the close of the day, when many noble knights lay dead on the field.

At last King Arthur smote Sir Modred under his shield. When Sir Modred felt it was his death-wound, he struck the king's helmet such a mighty blow that his sword pierced it and wounded King Arthur on the head. Then Sir Modred fell dead, and the noble Arthur fell in a swoon to the earth.

When King Arthur came to himself, he called feebly for Sir Bedivere, one of his knights.

"Take my good sword, Excalibur," said the king, "and haste you to yonder water. When you come there, throw the sword into the water, and return to me and tell me what you shall have seen. I have a grievous wound, and my time is not long."

Sir Bedivere departed. On his way to the place, the knight looked upon the richly jeweled sword, which grew brighter the more he looked upon it, and he thought that no good would come from throwing the sword into the water. So he hid it under a tree and returned to the king, who asked:

"What saw you there?"

"Sir," said the knight, "I saw nothing but the water rise and fall."

"That is untruly said," cried the king. "Go, therefore, and do as I bid you. As you are dear to me, save not the sword, but throw it into the water."

Again Sir Bedivere departed, and took the sword in his hand. Again he thought it a sin to throw away the noble sword. Again he hid it, and again he returned to the king and told him he had obeyed his command.

"What saw you there?" asked King Arthur.

"Sir," said he, "I saw nothing but the water rise and fall."

"You are untrue, indeed!" exclaimed the king; "for you have betrayed me twice. You are called a noble knight, and would betray me for a jeweled sword! Haste again to the water's edge, for your delay puts me in great danger. If you obey not my command, and I shall ever see you more, I shall slay you with my own hand. You would see me dead for my jeweled sword."

Once more Sir Bedivere came to the edge of the water. He took the sword up, and bound the girdle about the hilt, and threw it into the water as far as he could. As he did so, there rose an arm above the water and caught the sword and shook it three times. Then the hand disappeared beneath the water with the sword.

Once more Sir Bedivere returned to King Arthur and told him all he had seen.

"Ah, me!" said Arthur, feebly; "help me to the water's edge, for I fear I have tarried too long already."

Then the knight carried the dying king on his back to the edge of the water, where appeared a barge with fair ladies in it. Among them were three queens, who wept when they saw their king. One of the queens was King Arthur's sister, who cried:

"Why have you tarried so long, dear brother? That wound on your head is grievous."

A Statue of King Arthur at Innsbruck

As the barge moved away from the shore, and Sir Bedivere saw his king being borne away, he cried:

"My lord! Arthur! What shall I do now that you go from me?"

"Grieve not," said King Arthur, "and do as well as you may. I go to the Vale of Avalon—

> "Where falls not hail, nor rain, nor any snow,
>   Nor ever the wind blows loudly; but it lies
> Deep-meadow'd, happy, fair with orchard lawns
> And bowery billows crown'd with a summer sea,
>   Where I will heal me of my grievous wound."
>   ~TENNYSON— *The Passing of Arthur*

Thus did the knight see King Arthur borne away in the ship in which were the three queens, and he saw him no more.

Some say that King Arthur lives still, with his knights and companions, in an enchanted castle, and that he shall come again to rule. Others declare that on his tomb is written:

"Here Arthur lies, king once and king to be."

ROLAND

My friend, my Roland, God guard thy soul!
Never on earth such knight hath been.
~John O'Hagan

ROLAND SEES THE KING

Charlemagne, or the Great Charles, was a powerful king of France. He had in his vast kingdom many noble knights whose brave deeds have been told again and again, ever since they were first sung by the minstrel at the famous battle of Hastings in England, a thousand years ago.

Roland was a little beggar-lad. He lived with his mother near the forest of this king's country, where he gathered the nuts for food.

"When you first see King Charlemagne," Roland's mother had often said to him, "it will be the beginning of a new life for you. You will be a beggar-boy no longer."

Roland was just twelve years old when he first saw the king— and this was the way it happened: It was known that Charlemagne and his army were to be entertained at a castle in Italy. Roland, hearing this, and remembering his mother's words, was eager to catch a glimpse of the man who was to change his life. He hastened to a hillside that overlooked the road along which the king and his men were expected to pass. Roland's only companion was Oliver, the son of the governor of the town. The two boys climbed the hillside, and there watched anxiously for the approach of their hero. Poor Roland's head and limbs were bare. His patched, scanty clothing was a strange contrast to Oliver's rich dress of a court page.

"I am sure they are coming!" shouted Roland. "I see a light among the trees. I think it must be the flashing of the sun upon their bright armor. It grows brighter and brighter as they come near."

Very soon the noise of the tramping of many feet was heard, and the rustling of dry leaves in the wood — then a cloud of dust rose above the trees. The bright shields and glittering war-coats were seen in the distance. The beggar-boy leaned forward to see the king and his army in battle array. First came the heralds of the king, who bore the banner of France. Then followed messengers, a body of guards, and a long line of bishops and priests.

"See, Roland!" cried Oliver, "that must be the king himself." Roland knew it was King Charlemagne, for who else could bear himself so proudly and so nobly?

The two lads were so filled with admiration, they could scarcely speak. When the last gay banner had disappeared, Roland told Oliver that some day they should both be knights and ride to battle with the king. Together, by the roadside, the boys knelt, and promised to be true to each other, and to the king, as long as they should live.

As the boys rose from their knees, they sealed their promise by exchanging gifts. Oliver took from his belt a richly carved dagger, while Roland drew forth from his ragged garment a rusty old sword-blade.

Thus Roland and Oliver parted at the close of that eventful day when they first saw Charlemagne, whose faithful knights they afterward became.

Roland, filled with joy, hurried to his poor dwelling, and rushing into his mother's arms, exclaimed:

"Mother, I have seen the king! — his knights and his peers. Would I were a knight, that I, too, might go forth to war."

Roland begged to know the secret of his life— and this is what he learned: His mother was the Princess Bertha; his father was a gallant count; and King Charlemagne, whose fame was known in all lands, was his uncle. Roland wept for joy. He bade his mother good-by, and believing that the new life had already begun, he hastened to demand his rights of the King of France.

Charlemagne and the peers of the realm were dining at the governor's castle. The courts and halls were filled with knights and squires. They talked of war, of chivalry, and of heroism. Above the voices of the feasters were heard the strains of sweet music.

Suddenly, in the midst of the feast, Roland, with proud step and flashing eye, entered the banquet- hall.

The king, surprised to see a half-clad boy thus interrupt the royal feast, exclaimed:

"Is not the forest a better place for you, my boy, than this castle at a royal feast?"

"The slave eats the nuts in the forest," answered Roland, proudly; "and the peasant drinks the clear water from the brook; but the best things on your table belong to my mother."

Charlemagne smiled at the boy's reply, and said:

"Your mother must be a grand lady, indeed. Has she servants? Has she a carver and a cup-bearer? Has she soldiers, watchmen, and minstrels?"

"She has, indeed," the lad replied: "my two arms are her soldiers; my eyes are her watchmen; my lips are her minstrels. I should like you to see my mother, who dwells in the forest."

The king was as much puzzled as he was delighted with the child's answers. After Roland left the dining-hall, Charlemagne turned to Malagis, the dwarf, and asked:

"What think you of this strange boy, who has dared interrupt our feast? Has he not a kingly bearing, in spite of his tattered garments?"

"My lord," said the dwarf, "I think the lad belongs not in the forest, but in the palace; for I believe that kings are his ancestors, and that royal blood flows through his veins. He will perform great deeds in the years to come. Let no harm come to him. Have him brought before you again. I see by the stars that, somehow, his life and yours are strangely mingled."

Immediately the king sent his squires to bring the boy and his mother to the castle. When they appeared before the king, he saw that Roland's mother was the Lady Bertha, his own sister, who had married against his wishes and been banished with her husband from the kingdom.

Charlemagne's joy was great. He ordered a feast to be prepared in their honor, and Roland sat at the right hand of the king. The lad was made a page in the service of a duke. His ragged clothes were exchanged for a rich gown of velvet and gold. He was no longer Roland the beggar-lad, who gathered nuts in the forest, but Roland, the nephew of the great King of France.

ROLAND BECOMES A KNIGHT

Some of Roland's ancestors were the noblest heroes the world had ever seen. As the dwarf in the king's court had said, surely the blood of heroes flowed in the lad's veins. Of all the knights and warriors in Charlemagne's kingdom, Roland was the bravest and most skillful. When he reached manhood, it was right he should have suitable armor as a knight of the king. His armor was so wondrously wrought that some said it was made for him by Vulcan, the blacksmith of the Golden Age. His helmet was made of steel, inlaid with pearls, and engraved on it were strange words and battle-scenes. The metal had been taken from the earth by the dwarf-folk who lived in the North. When Roland first put on the helmet, his comrades said:

"What need has he of such wonderful armor? It would be better to give it to someone who has not a charmed life."

Roland's shield was made of steel, copper, and gold. His spurs had once belonged to King Arthur when he and his Knights of the Round Table dwelt on the earth. They were given to Roland by the fairy-queen of Avalon, where King Arthur had gone to be healed of his grievous wound.

In the days when Roland lived, heroes had names for their swords. Roland called his sword Durandal, which surpassed his uncle's sword, and even the famous Excalibur, that King Arthur received from the Lady of the Lake. This sword had been carried by Hector in the battles with the Greeks. There were strange letters on one side of it, which no one but the dwarf could read:

"Let honor he to him who most deserveth it." On the other side of it were the words: "I am Durandal, which Trojan Hector wore."

Some thought that an angel or a fairy had given the sword to Charlemagne, and told him to gird it on a young knight who had never known reproach or fear. However that may have been, Roland prized this sword beyond measure. Next to it, he cared most for his famous ivory horn, which hung from his neck by a gold chain. It was set with precious gems and inlaid with silver and gold. No one in the kingdom had ever been able to blow upon this horn. Knights had come from far and near to try; but no one had succeeded. When Roland became a knight,

Charlemagne was anxious to give the horn to him, and bade him try to blow a blast, saying:

"My dear nephew, you have never yet been conquered in a battle, nor have you failed in anything you have undertaken. Here is that which will test your strength. It is the horn of my grandfather. In his days, when men were stronger and seemingly more valiant than now, the most wondrous sounds were made to come forth from it. Men have grown wondrous weak of lungs, — not a man in all France can blow the horn now."

When the king had finished speaking, Roland took the horn, looked at it, put it to his lips, and blew.

There came forth a sound more wonderful than any one there had ever heard. It resounded through the halls of the great palace, out into the streets, over hills and mountains, and through the forest.

When the people heard it they were astonished. Some thought the end of the world had come. Others thought it was thunder filled with music.

"I give you this horn," said the king to Roland, "for you have won it fairly. No one can ever doubt your right to it. I give it to you on one condition, that you shall never blow it save in time of battle and in great distress."

When Roland had received the horn, he was fully armed as a knight for battle, with his shield and helmet, his trusty sword, and his wonderful horn.

ROLAND LOSES HIS LIFE

CHARLEMAGNE, with his brave knights, had conquered so many countries that his kingdom stretched in all directions. He had crossed the high mountains between France and Spain, and destroyed the beautiful cities of the Spanish Moors. The French king was getting ready to return home, when he remembered that one city remained unconquered.

Marsilius, the Moorish king, fearing that this beloved city would be destroyed also, sent to Charlemagne and begged for terms of peace.

"What think you of those offers of peace from the Moorish king?" said Charlemagne to his peers and knights. "These are his promises. Will he keep them?"

"No, no," answered Roland, "you have trusted him before and he has been untrue to you."

Then Ganelon, Roland's stepfather, urged Charlemagne to put an end to the war, and send one of his barons to Marsilius to accept the offers of peace. To this all the other knights agreed, and the king asked:

"Whom shall we send on this dangerous errand?"

Immediately Roland begged that he might be the messenger; but his faithful friend Oliver interrupted him, and urged that he might be the one to go.

Charlemagne silenced them both, and said that none of his twelve peers should go. At last Roland said to his uncle that he thought Ganelon would be the best one to carry the messages— to which all agreed.

When Ganelon heard that it was the king's wish that he should go, he mounted his horse and unwillingly started on his journey to the Moorish king. Now he believed that Roland, whom he hated, had done this out of spite, and he determined to have his revenge. So when he delivered the king's message to Marsilius, he exchanged promises with him as to the best plan of overtaking and destroying Charlemagne's rear-guard, of which Roland would be in charge, as it went through the mountain pass. For if Roland were slain, the hosts of the French king would soon disappear. Then Ganelon took the noblest hostages (persons held as a pledge in war) in the land, the richest treasures, and the keys of the great city, and returned to the king, who waited for him.

Charlemagne rejoiced when he received the message of peace from Marsilius. Clarions were sounded throughout the camp. The tents were folded; the pack-horses and mules were loaded; the knights mounted their horses. With banners waving, the army started for their beloved France, which lay just beyond the mountains.

"Who shall take charge of our rear-guard," said Charlemagne, "while we pass safely through the gates of the city?"

"Roland, your nephew," said Ganelon, the traitor; "no one is more worthy than he."

To this the king agreed at once. Roland put on his matchless armor, laced his helmet, and girded on his famous sword. Then, asking his uncle for his own special bow, he mounted his horse and rode back to the rear-guard. His comrades and twenty thousand fighting men rode with him.

While Charlemagne dreamed strange dreams of Ganelon, the army of the enemy was filling the valleys. The French army entered the pass in the mountains called the Vale of Thorns — a narrow, rugged gorge, with dark rocks on both sides.

Suddenly a thousand trumpets blared forth from the valley below— a sound that struck terror to the heart of every Frenchman who heard it.

"Roland," cried Oliver, "I fear we are followed by the enemy."

"Be it so," answered Roland; "and may we win the victory."

The faithful Oliver climbed upon a hill from which he could look far down the valley. There he saw the hosts of the Moorish king in the passes, the groves, and the valleys. He cried in amazement to Roland to sound upon his horn, that Charlemagne might return and give them help. Roland would not do so, but said:

"The king left us here with twenty thousand men, and he thinks every man of us a hero. No, my good sword and I shall fight it out."

Thus Roland and Oliver waited on the hillside for the enemy, as they had waited years before for their king. The good archbishop blessed the host as they knelt on the ground. Then, with Roland at their head, they faced the foe, into whose hands they had been betrayed.

It was a terrible battle. Roland, Oliver, the archbishop, and all the knights fought bravely. At first the French seemed to gain; but Marsilius urged his men to fight until Roland should be slain. Then he appeared with fresh troops, and hemmed the heroes in on all sides. The pass was so narrow that the living trampled on the wounded, the dying, and the dead. All customs of war, all rules of chivalry, were forgotten in the desperate struggle for victory.

When Roland saw his brave knights falling, one by one, he cried:

"*I will sound my horn.* It may be the king will hear it and return."

He raised the horn to his lips, and sounded such a mighty blast that Charlemagne, who was thirty leagues away, heard it and cried:

"It is Roland's horn! He would never have sounded it if he were not hard pressed in battle."

A second and a third time the sound of the horn was heard. Then one of the dukes cried:

"It is Roland! Someone has betrayed him, and there is a battle. Let us make haste to the rescue. Oh, king, it is Roland's cry of distress we hear."

Ganelon tried to deceive the king, who had him seized, bound, and made a prisoner. Then Charlemagne and his knights hastened to Roland and the rear-guard. They rode over high mountains and through deep valleys. All the horns, trumpets, and bugles were sounded at once, that Roland might know the king was coming.

Brave Roland heard the sound and gave thanks. The enemy heard it also, and they were filled with fear.

Roland and Oliver were both wounded. When Roland saw his dear friend fall, calling to him for help, he thought it was the end. Oliver became delirious. Not knowing what he was doing, he struck at Roland, who cried:

"I am Roland, who loves you as his life."

"I hear your voice," said Oliver; "but I cannot see you. Was it you I struck?"

"I forgive you," said Roland; "you did not hurt me."

The two friends embraced each other, and thus was their parting made. Roland, thinking he had not long to live after his friend had been taken, went up "a little hill that lies toward Spain." For the last time he sounded the horn. Feeble as it was, Charlemagne heard it — for he was already in the mountain pass; but he knew it was the blast of a dying man.

Then, with great effort, Roland took his sword, Durandal, fearing it would fall into the hands of the enemy, and crawled on his hands and knees to a huge rock—

> And on the slimy stone he struck the blade with might —
> The bright hilt, sounding, shook, the blade flash'd sparks of light;
> Wildly again he struck, and his sick head went round,
> Again there sparkled fire, again rang hollow sound;
> Ten times he struck, and threw strange echoes down the glade,
> Yet still *unbroken*, sparkling fire, glitter' d the peerless blade.
> ~BUCHANAN— *Death of Roland*

Roland turned his face toward Spain, to tell, in this silent way, that he fell like a conqueror. He thought of his beloved king, his family, and his friends in France. Then the brave knight raised his right-hand glove as a sign of surrender — Roland was dead!

Charlemagne arrived soon after, but too late to save the life of his beloved nephew. He lifted Roland tenderly in his arms, and cried:

"My faithful Roland! bravest of men! noblest of knights! how shall I tell them in France that you lie dead in Spain?"

ST. DENIS

In former times it was my fatal chance
To be the proudest maiden ever known.
By birth I was the daughter of a king,
Though now a breathless tree and senseless thing.

St. Denis is the patron or guardian saint of France, as St. George is of England. Among the many strange stories told about him is the following:

St. Denis once found himself spellbound in a desolate land. There was no way of escape; he had nothing to eat except herbs and fruit, and no companion except his horse. As the wretched man wandered wearily from one spot to another of the wilderness, he discovered a tree which bore purple fruit. This was unfortunate for St. Denis, for it seems that the tree was enchanted. Its berries, which he ate, had the power to change him into a hart. He looked into a pool nearby, and in its clear surface beheld himself. His body, once tall and erect, was bent to earth and covered with coarse hair; his head, once crowned with a steel helmet and waving plumes, now carried a pair of horns; his eyes, once filled with a look of pride and courage, now had the frightened gaze of a deer.

St. Denis knew it must be the fruit that had changed him so. He hastened to the enchanted tree, where he fell upon the ground and complained bitterly. All at once, he was startled to hear groans coming from the tree under which he was lying. He listened, and heard distinctly a strange, sweet voice. It was the voice of Eglantine, the king's daughter, who bade the poor knight grieve no more, and then she told him her story.

The maiden was the king's daughter, she said; but was being punished for her overbearing pride. For seven long years she must be imprisoned in the hollow of the tree. During that time, the knight, also, must remain in the shape of a hart. At the end of that time, if by means of a purple rose the knight regained his former shape, he would have the power to set her free.

The poor knight listened again for the voice, but no sound came from the tree. He waited and waited, counting the years by the seasons, as they came and went; by the flowers, as they bloomed and faded.

During all the long, weary years the knight's only companion was his faithful horse.

The seven years passed. One day, the trusty horse left the poor dumb hart asleep at the foot of the enchanted tree. He wandered over a very high mountain, where he found beautiful roses in bloom. He plucked a branch of roses and carried it to his master.

As soon as the knight beheld the sweet-perfumed flowers, he remembered that by means of a purple rose he was to become himself again. He ate the beautiful flowers, and fell into a peaceful and refreshing sleep. For a whole day the knight slept, while the rain fell on his hairy coat and washed it all away. The horns disappeared, as well as every trace of the change that had come over him.

When morning dawned, there appeared, lying asleep

under the enchanted tree, not a timid hart, but a valiant knight, and by his side a faithful horse kept watch.

After a while St. Denis wakened slowly; but he could not believe that he was himself again. When he found it was true, he gave thanks. Then he called to his horse, now grown old and forlorn, and stroked his shaggy mane until it fell in soft waves again, and the hair of his body became smooth as silk once more.

Then the knight examined his armor and his helmet, and put them in order, as befitted a knight of France. When all was done, St. Denis stood beside the enchanted tree. He thought of Eglantine, the king's daughter, and of her last words to him:

> "When this is done be sure you cut in twain
> This fatal tree wherein I do remain."

The brave champion of France was not one to forget to help another in distress. With one stroke of his trusty sword, he struck the tree, which parted to the roots.

There was a sudden flash of fire, followed by dark clouds of smoke. When all had ceased, there came forth from the hollow of the tree the fair maid Eglantine, with her eyes looking meekly on the ground.

"Fair maid," said the knight, "I know not whether you are angel or fairy obliged for some punishment to be thus imprisoned in the hollow of this tree in the forest. Tell me, I pray, who you are, what is your fault, and if I may not serve you?"

The fair Eglantine, from whose face every trace of haughtiness had disappeared, related again how she was the king's daughter who had been punished because she was so proud. Then she begged St. Denis, very humbly, to take her to her father's kingdom, where she had been mourned as dead.

Then St. Denis — for he was a noble knight — promised that he would take the maid in safety to her home.

So the knight and Eglantine traveled for many, many days. At length they arrived at the palace, where there was great surprise and rejoicing. The happy king folded his child in his arms, and then welcomed the strange knight who had brought her safely home.

When his faithful horse had been well cared for, the knight, being weary, laid aside his heavy armor and rested. There was a great feast of welcome given by the king in his palace. When St. Denis again beheld the maiden whom he had rescued from the tree in the forest, she was dressed all in white and attended by many fair maidens. She was no longer the nymph of the woodland, but Eglantine, the daughter of the king.

THE CID

How much of my young heart, O Spain,
Went out to thee in days of yore!
What dreams romantic filled my brain.
And summoned back to life again
The Paladins of Charlemagne,
The Cid Campeador!
~Longfellow— *Castles in Spain*

Spain's great hero, the Cid, who lived several hundred years ago, was quite different from most of the other heroes one reads about. Many curious tales have been written about him, which may or may not be true. However, he was a great fighter, which made a man a hero in those days, when nobles and knights slept with their war-horses near them, ready for battle. Whether in single combat or at the head of an army, this hero was victorious always. He was obeyed by his followers, and feared by his enemies.

Once he captured five Moorish kings, and when he gave them their freedom they called him "Cid," which means conqueror or champion. The word "Sid," which signifies master, is used still in some Eastern countries.

Rodrigo Diaz, or Ruy Diaz, which was the Cid's real name, was only a lad when he fearlessly struck down a count for having insulted his father, who was too feeble to resent the injury himself.

This count had a daughter named Ximena, who was anxious to have revenge on the young man for having slain her father. So she appealed to the king many times, but without success. Rodrigo was now too famous a fighter for the king to have him punished in any way. Each time Dona Ximena went to court to demand his punishment, she heard more of the wonderful conquests the Cid had made, and at last she grew to admire his courage and strength.

The last time the maiden appealed to the king, it was not to have the Cid punished; but— what do you think? —she asked that she should be made his wife.

The king, being greatly pleased at the pleasant turn of affairs, sent for the Cid, and told him what was the lady's desire. Whereupon the Cid went to the palace, with three hundred attendants, all gaily dressed, and with bright new armor. The marriage was celebrated with great splendor, as you may imagine. The Cid was dressed in handsome black satin, with a gorgeous cloak and feathered cap; his sword, Tizona, was fastened at his side. The bride wore a richly embroidered gown, high-heeled shoes of red leather, and a necklace of gold.

The wedding procession marched through the streets, which were festooned gaily as for a holiday. After the marriage a grand dinner was given, at which the minstrel sang in honor of the bride and groom.

The Cid's favorite horse was Babieca, which means "Booby." Now "Booby" was so fearless and so faithful to his master that he deserved a better name. It is interesting to learn how the Cid came by this horse. It seems that when Rodrigo was quite young, he asked his father to give him a colt. He was told to take his choice of all the horses that were feeding in the field. Rodrigo, pointing to a half-starved colt, cried:

"I will choose this one."

"Not Babieca!" exclaimed his father, with surprise; "a poor choice, indeed!"

But the lad would have no other. He was sure "Booby" would make a fine horse some day, and he did. The colt soon learned to obey his young master, and to fear nothing.

For many years the Cid served the king, fighting and conquering the Moors, who had come over from the northern part of Africa and taken a great part of Spain. It happened, however, that this mighty hero displeased the king, who sent him out of the kingdom. The Cid, feeling very sure his sovereign would need him and send for him before long, obeyed the unjust sentence. He bade goodbye to his wife and his two daughters, and with sixty followers he left his home.

There is a strange story told of the Cid, which is not much to his credit. He was greatly in need of money; so he pledged two large chests, which he pretended were full of gold, to some money-lenders who gave him the money, keeping the chests as security until the debt should be paid. But, sad to relate, when the reckoning day came and it was not paid, the money- lenders opened the heavy chests, and found them filled with— sand!

The Cid was right in thinking the king would need him. He conquered many of his enemies, from whom he secured a great deal of booty. A large part of this he sent to the king, who recalled him at once. Many times was the Cid banished or sent away; but as many times was he recalled, having been victorious. At last the king found he could not get along, in fighting his foes, without his champion.

The Cid's two daughters married two young counts. It was not long after their grand wedding that the Cid found out what cowards his sons-in-law were,

— and if there was anyone he disliked, it was a coward.

One day it chanced that a lion, breaking loose from his keepers, rushed into the hall where the counts were playing chess and the Cid was sleeping:

> Lo, loud outcries rent the palace,
>   Shook its walls and turrets high!
> "Ware the lion! ware the lion!
>   He is loose!" was heard the cry.

The counts fled in great haste— one fell headlong into a vat, and the other hid behind the couch where the Cid lay asleep. The conqueror, who feared neither man nor beast, rose quickly, and, taking his sword in one hand, grasped the lion by the mane with the other, and put him back in his cage. Then he returned to his couch and asked for his sons-in-law. One was pulled from his hiding-place behind the couch, while the other was dragged from the vat. The Cid asked impatiently:

"Had you no weapons, that you fled in such haste?"

The counts made no answer, but vowed to have their revenge later. They were too much afraid of the man who had faced the lion to try to do him harm.

So, instead, they treated their wives, the Cid's daughters, most cruelly, and left them in the forest to starve. Fortunately, one of the Cid's servants found them, and hastened to tell his master.

As soon as the Cid heard it, he ordered the counts to appear before the assembly and answer for their cruel and cowardly conduct. He challenged them to fight; but they made excuses for themselves by saying that his daughters were not as high-born as they. Needless to say, they were properly beaten, and fled from the country. In the meantime, two princes who were of higher blood than the counts asked to marry the daughters of the Cid.

Some years later, the Moors returned to besiege that part of the country still guarded by the Cid and his followers. The hero was getting ready to meet his old enemy once more, when it was said that he saw a vision which made him think he should not live much longer. So he gave instructions that, when he was dead, none of his men should know it, lest by their grief the Moors should find it out. He told his comrades to embalm his body, and added:

> "Saddle next my Babieca,
>   Arm him well as for the fight;
> On his back then tie my body,
>   In my well-known armor dight."
>
> "In my right hand place Tizona;
>   Lead me forth into the war;
> Bear my standard fast behind me,
>   As it was my wont of yore."
> ~*Ancient Spanish Ballads* (Lockhart's Tr.)

When the Cid died, all his wishes were carried out. His faithful knights fastened his body on his beloved horse, and tied his feet to the stirrups. Silently he rode in amid them. The Moors knew not that the Cid was dead. They were terrified when they beheld him, and fled in confusion and dismay. Many of them were slain. Although the Christians had taken the city, they knew they could not keep it without their brave leader. Silently they marched out of the city; their dead commander, dressed for battle, still at the head of his army.

The Moors lingered around the city for several days, but

dared not pass through the gates, which were open. When they did so, they were greatly astonished to find a notice of the Cid's death, and that the Christians had fled.

According to the king's orders, the Cid was dressed in his finest robes (given to him by the Sultan of Turkey because of his many victories) and placed in the great convent at Cardeña. There the hero was left for ten years in the chair of state, with his sword by his side. His faithful wife, Ximena, watched over him as long as she lived.

No one was allowed to mount Babieca after the Cid's death; and when the good horse died, he was buried at the gate of the church, near his master.

While we cannot believe all that has been said and sung of this powerful hero, we can understand how he came to be thought of by his countrymen as the

> Mighty victor, never vanquish'd,
>   Bulwark of our native land,
> Shield of Spain, her boast and glory,
>   Knight of the far-dreaded brand.

THE UNKNOWN ISLAND

...The isle is full of noises,
Sounds and sweet airs, that give delight and hurt not.
Sometimes a thousand twangling instruments
Will hum about mine ears, and sometimes voices,
That, if I then had wak'd after long sleep,
Will make me sleep again: and then, in dreaming,
The clouds, methought, would open and show riches
Ready to drop upon me; that, when I wak'd,
I cried to dream again.
~Shakespeare— *The Tempest*

I. THE PILOT'S STORY

Before Columbus appeared at the court of Spain and told his marvelous tale of an unknown land beyond the sea, an old storm-tossed pilot arrived, one day, in Lisbon, on the coast of Portugal.

In those days the people, especially those who lived near the coast, were filled with a restless spirit of adventure and discovery. Every story of unknown lands, of strange people or hidden treasures, found ready listeners.

A crowd of eager followers gathered around the bewildered old sailor. He told them of an unknown island to which he had been driven by a violent storm. On this island were beautiful cities, where Christians lived, who seemed to know nothing of the rest of the world, — and surely the rest of the world knew nothing of them. They told the old man that they were the descendants of the Christians who were driven out of Spain when that country was conquered by the Moors —those wild folk who had come over from Africa and taken possession of a large part of Spain, which they ruled for several hundred years. They asked the stranger, who was their first visitor, many questions about their native land. They were grieved when they heard their old enemy still ruled their beloved country. Then they urged him to go to church with them, that he might know all they had told him was true. The old man would not do so, but hurried to his ship and set sail. No sooner had he started than a terrible storm arose. He lost control of his vessel and was carried far out to sea. He looked everywhere for the mysterious island he had visited, but it was nowhere to be seen.

The people of Portugal were much excited when they heard the old pilot's story. They did not know what to make of it. Finally, some of the wiser ones remembered having read in the old records that when Spain was conquered by the Moors there were seven bishops who had led seven bands of Christians to some distant shore, where they hoped to found Christian cities and live in peace.

Nothing had ever been heard of them. Even the story of their exile had been almost forgotten until the old sailor reminded them of it by his strange adventure.

"Perhaps," said they, "this is the very Island of the Seven Cities, where the good bishops and their faithful followers went so long ago."

II. THE YOUNG CAVALIER

OF all the believers in the wondrous story, no one was more interested or thrilled than a young cavalier or knight of the court of Portugal named Don Fernando. He was a great favorite with the people, for he was not only the leader in all their sports and amusements, but brave and true as well. He became so interested in the story that he could think of nothing else day or night. At last he fitted out an expedition to search for this wonder of the sea, and satisfy his curiosity.

When Don Fernando was ready to sail, the king said to him:

"I will make you the governor of any land you may discover, if you will pay all the expenses of the voyage and give one tenth of the profits to the crown."

This the young man agreed to do. With his two vessels he steered in the direction of the Canary Islands, where the old man had said the mysterious island lay.

It was not long after he had started that a dreadful storm arose, and mighty seas broke over the decks. The two vessels, which were driven hither and thither, were separated. The frightened sailors thought there was no hope of being saved.

Suddenly the storm ceased, the ocean became calm, and the dark clouds passed away. The sailors on board the ship with Don Fernando saw in the distance a beautiful island rise out of the vanishing darkness. On it were stately cities with high walls and lordly castles.

In vain the pilot looked for such an island on his maps: he could find none.

Had they lost their way? Was it the island of the old pilot's story that lay before them?

As they gazed, they saw a richly carved barge coming toward them. The rowers of the barge were dressed in a quaint style of an age long gone by. They sang an old Spanish song as they rowed with their gaily painted oars, keeping time with the music. Slowly they drew near till the barge was abreast of the ship.

In the barge sat a gaily dressed cavalier. Over his head waved a banner of the cross. When the barge reached Don Fernando's vessel, the old hidalgo, for such he was, welcomed the storm-tossed stranger to the— Island of the Seven Cities.

Don Fernando could scarcely believe his eyes or his ears, and cried:

"Is it true that the storm has driven me just where I wanted to go? Is this the place that I have dreamed of day and night for so long a time?"

He could not doubt it longer, for the cavalier, after asking him his name and his errand to the island, said:

"This is our festival which we celebrate in honor of the escape of our ancestors from the Moors who took our beloved country. You have come at the right time, indeed."

When Don Fernando had made himself known, as well as his agreement with the king of his country, the cavalier said he should be made governor of the island.

Accordingly, Don Fernando was taken into the quaint barge, and rowed to the shore of the island. What a strange place he saw! Everything seemed to have gone back hundreds of years!

As they passed, the queer-looking soldiers on guard at the different posts asked who it was that passed, and every time the same answer came :

"The Governor of the Seven Cities"

Strange to say, Don Fernando was soon acknowledged governor without surprise or question. He spent a short time at the courthouse, then joined in the festivities, which he greatly enjoyed.

When the time arrived for him to return to his vessel, he was sorry indeed to leave the island, where he had been received so graciously and pleasantly.

He entered the barge, which started in the direction of his vessel, but there was no vessel to be seen! Had it been carried out to sea?

Whether it had or not, Don Fernando soon forgot all about it. He was soothed by the sound of the oars in the water, as the gaily dressed rowers kept time with the singing of the old Spanish song. Everything seemed to fade before his eyes as the old cavalier called:

"Good Night, Governor of the Seven Cities!"

III. A STRANGER IN HIS HOME

Don Fernando knew nothing more until he found himself in the cabin of a strange vessel, surrounded by strange faces, and he cried:

"What does it all mean? Where am I?"

"On board a vessel bound for Lisbon, by which you were taken from a drifting wreck," was the answer.

When the vessel reached his native city, Don Fernando hastened to his old home, where he expected to receive his usual welcome. The porter at the door knew nothing of the stranger or his family.

In despair, the wanderer hurried to the home of his lady-love, whom he had left when he went in search of that wonder of the sea.

"She will know me, I am sure," he said to himself, as he called her name again and again. But no, she turned from him in haste and left the balcony, where he saw her as of old.

Don Fernando was not to be dismissed in this fashion, however, and insisted upon seeing the lady. As the porter opened the door cautiously he rushed in, and never stopped until he had thrown himself at the lady's feet, and declared she was his lady-love, and asked if it was not her portrait that hung on the wall.

You may imagine the cavalier's surprise and dismay when the lady said, as she pointed to the picture, that he must be talking of her great-grandmother.

Alas! like poor Rip Van Winkle, when he came down from the mountains after his long sleep, Don Fernando was a stranger in his native land — even in his old home. No one knew him or believed in his tale of the wonderful island, with its stately cities, high walls, and lordly castles. When he declared he had earned the title of governor of the island, the people thought he must be crazy or dreaming.

Many times Don Fernando wished himself back on the island — where he must have been at least a hundred years. Many times he dreamed of the gaily dressed cavalier in the quaint barge, of the rowers and their old Spanish song. How he longed to hear that song again!

IV. ST. BRANDAN'S ISLAND

Don Fernando would have started on another cruise, but he had no money. Finally, he was able to sail as far as the Canary Islands. There the people listened to his story with great interest. They believed he had seen St. Brandan's Island, that wonder of the sea, which they had always hoped to find.

They told him that this mysterious island had appeared to them many times; but when they went in search of it — there was nothing to be seen.

Strange to say, it was only when the weather was very clear that they could catch a glimpse of it.

There were many stories told of this mysterious island, which received its name from St. Brandan, who had gone there with some of his followers, many hundred years before, but never had returned.

It was said that they had found a giant buried on the island, whom they brought to life. They talked to him about the people who had lived there. When St.

Brandan found the giant willing and pleased to listen, he taught him something of the Christian religion.

The giant, however, did not seem to care to live, for after fifteen days he begged to be allowed to die again. It was said, also, that the giant told the visitors of an island, with walls of gold, that shone like crystal; but it had no entrance. He promised to guide them to it. So, taking the cable of the ship, he flung himself into the water. A fierce storm arose before they had gone very far. They were obliged to turn back without seeing the golden-walled island, and not long after their return the giant died.

Another story is that the priest prayed they might find land on Easter day. At that very time an unknown island seemed to rise out of the sea. He and his followers landed, and spent a short time there. When they set sail again, they looked back and saw the island plunge into the sea— for it was nothing more than a monstrous whale!

If you have read Charles Kingsley's charming story of The Water Babies, you will remember, perhaps, that St. Brandan's Isle was their home, where Tom went. The author tells how St. Brandan saw a golden island, one night at sunset, from his home on the Irish coast. He and his followers sailed in the direction of the fairy island, but they never returned.

St. Brandan found the island covered with cedars, in which the birds lodged. He began to preach to them, and they liked what he said much more than did the people whom he had left at home. Indeed, the birds liked to hear him preach so well that they repeated his words to the fishes.

And the fishes were so pleased to hear him that they told the Water Babies, whom he taught for hundreds of years— until he fell asleep— and he may be sleeping still.

At the end of the story, it was on St. Brandan's Isle that Tom found Ellie, who had been waiting for him for hundreds of years. Tom was so pleased to see Ellie, after all his long travels, and Ellie was so pleased to see Tom, after waiting for him so long— that they kept on looking at each other for seven years, and did not speak.

Whatever the truth may have been about this enchanted island, the people of the Canary Islands never gave up their belief that it would be found. They declared they had seen—

> The cloud-capp'd towers, the gorgeous palaces,
> The solemn temples.

They listened just as eagerly and with as much hope to each new tale of its discovery as they had listened to the old ones by which they had been enchanted— and disappointed.

V. THE FAITHFUL WATCHER

> But on still, clear summer evenings, when the sun sinks down into the sea, among the golden cloud capes, and cloud islands, and azure sky, the sailors fancy that they see, away to the westward, St. Brandan's fairly isle.
> ~Charles Kingsley— *The Water Babies*

When Don Fernando heard about this wonder of the sea, he was spellbound. He firmly believed he had seen St. Brandan's Island. Being unable to get farther than the Canary Islands, the disappointed cavalier went every day to the highest point of land overlooking the sea, and watched for the fairy island, which had appeared and disappeared so often. He hoped to see it once more, even though in the far distance. Day after day, until he grew old and gray, he gazed out to sea.

One day he went to the place as usual, but he did not return. The people found him dead on the spot where he had watched so long and so faithfully for the unknown island.

BRIAN BORU

Remember the glories of Brian, the brave,
    Though the days of the hero are o'er;
Though lost to Mononia and cold in his grave,
    He returns to Kinkora no more!
That star of the field, which so often has poured
    Its beam on the battle, is set;
But enough of its glory remains on each sword
    To light us to victory yet.
      ~Thomas Moore

BRIAN Boru, which means Brian of the Tribute, was a famous king of Ireland, where he ruled for many years. He is best remembered for his victories over the Danes, and for freeing Ireland forever from their fierce invasions.

It was the custom, in those olden times, for a boy to be brought up away from home. It so happened that this Irish lad was reared at the court of a neighboring king, where his early life was spent amid scenes of danger, strife, and war. He had a soldier's strength and a soldier's courage, and, more than all, he had a love for his country, and gloried in defending it.

When the period of training had passed, Brian returned to his father's palace. As he and his men rode along the banks of the river Shannon, the young Irish boy bade his herald sound his horn, that King Kennedy might know his son was returning.

Before the herald had time to do so, however, there came from behind a high rock a strange sound that startled them all. It seemed like some bad tidings.

What astonished them still more was the appearance of a fair maiden, whose long golden hair fell about her shoulders. Before Brian had time to speak, she called to him that she was no banshee or fairy come to frighten him, but his foster-sister, who wished to welcome him home after his long absence.

The fair maiden crossed the ford, and making a low bow to Brian, told him that his father, King Kennedy, was waiting anxiously to hear the sound of his horn. "Is it thus you would frighten me with your warning song at my homecoming?" said Brian.

"Surely, the terror of the Danes fears not a maiden's voice," said she, playfully.

Then the herald sounded the horn, and Brian and his men crossed the river to meet the king.

When they reached the palace there was great rejoicing, and a royal feast was given in honor of the lad's return. Scarcely had the songs of the minstrels and the music of the harp ceased, when word came that the Danes were plundering the Clan of Cas, of which King Kennedy was the leader.

As soon as the king heard it, he turned to the strong, brave boy at his side, and cried:

"It is well, my boy, that you have come; for we shall have need of brave men, strong arms, and stout hearts to meet this mighty foe."

While the chiefs were talking about what was best to do— fight or fly— Brian cried impatiently:

"Why do you hesitate? There is no time to be lost. Oh, father! let me stand at the Ford of Tribute, and I will hold out against these bold invaders."

Such words, coming from a boy, stirred the hearts of the people so that they shouted, and, with new courage, they rallied around their chiefs. They gathered on the banks of the river Shannon, where they saw the beacon-fires gleam from the hilltops about them.

It was a terrible battle. Kings, princes, and chiefs fell under the fierce attack of the enemy. Among them were

King Kennedy and two of his sons. During all the long day, the brave Irish lad held his place at the Ford of Tribute, keeping back the Danes as they tried to rush up the valley.

When the battle raged the fiercest, a boat was seen coming down the rapids, so the storytellers say. In it stood a golden-haired maiden, all in white. It was Brian's foster-sister bringing supplies to him in her little boat. The frightened Danes, seeing her, and hearing her song that rose above the noise of the battle, fled in dismay.

Brian's brother, Mahon, was made king in his father's place; but the brothers found they could not hold out longer against the Danes in open battle. So they left the banks of the river Shannon, and went far into the forest. There they lived like robber chiefs, and spent much of their time in plundering the Danes, who were successful all through the south of Ireland. Mahon soon tired of the wild life in the forest, however, and made peace with the enemy. But Brian would not yield.

> First to face the foreign foe,
> First to strike the battle's blow;
> First to turn from triumph back,
> Last to leave the battle's wrack.
> ~Thomas Moore

Brian kept up his fierce attacks on the Danes until he became the terror of the country; but he was often sad and down-hearted. He saw his men fall one by one, until he had only a few left. One day, as before, he heard a voice calling him to leave his forest life and come home again. It was his foster-sister; she was the only one who dared carry the message telling him that his brother, Mahon, wanted to see him.

The young chieftain risked being captured by the Danes, and met his brother, whom he roused to strike another blow for freedom. Again the beacon-fires gleamed from the hilltops, all around. Again the chiefs of the Clan of Cas gathered under their banners and fought for freedom.

Finally, the Danish king of Limerick sent his herald to Mahon, and bade him give up his fortress, disband his men, and send the outlaw Brian to Limerick in chains and pay tribute to him. "We pay no tribute for that which is ours by right," answered Mahon. Brian would not yield.

> No, Freedom! whose smile we shall never resign,
>   Go, tell our invaders, the Danes,
> 'T is sweeter to bleed for an age at thy shrine,
>   Than to sleep but a moment in chains.
>   ~Thomas Moore

The brave brothers fought a great battle. Brian led and won it, routing the Danes as far as Limerick, which he captured instead of being taken there a captive.

When Mahon died, Brian was made king of three counties, and, later, of all Ireland. During his long and prosperous reign, he did much for his country and his people. He was kind and generous to his subjects, who loved him as much as his enemies feared him.

Brian lived to be a very, very old man. During the last battle with his old enemy, the Danes, at Clontarf, the aged Irish king was killed while waiting anxiously in his tent to know the result of the battle.

The Danes were completely routed, and Ireland was freed from their invasions ever after.

THE MONK AND THE BIRD'S SONG

> A hundred years had passed,
> And had not seemed so long
> As a single hour!
> ~Longfellow —*The Golden Legend.*

Long, long ago, there was a monk named Felix, who lived with other monks in an old convent. One morning this good man went alone into the forest to read and pray. In the book which he carried he read the following words:

> For a thousand years in thy sight
> Are but as yesterday when it is past,
> And as a watch in the night.
> ~Psalm XC. 4,

The sun shone through the trees, sending its golden rays into the dark forest; the wildflowers and creeping vines sent forth fragrant odors, filling the summer air with sweetness; the boughs of the giant trees whispered a gentle benediction. But Felix heeded not all these things, so intent was he, thinking of the words he had read but could not understand.

"How can a thousand years seem but as a day even to God himself?" asked the monk.

While deep in thought, he heard suddenly the song of a little bird very near him. The bird, which was snow-white, flew from tree to tree, singing as it went.

"I never heard anything so beautiful!" exclaimed Felix, as he followed after the bird.

It was as if a thousand harp-strings were ringing their clear, sweet notes through the woodland.

The bewildered monk dropped his book.

> He listened to the song,
> And hardly breathed or stirred,
> Until he saw, as in a vision,
> The land Elysian,
> And in the heavenly city heard
> Angelic feet
> Fall on the flagging of the street.
> And he would fain
> Have caught the wondrous bird,
> But strove in vain;
> For it flew away, away,
> Far over hill and dell.
> ~Longfellow— *The Golden Legend*

As Felix saw the sunlight fade, the shadows deepen, and heard the notes of the song grow faint, he knew that he must return to the convent. Sadly he turned his steps toward home, for he would have listened longer to the sweet music. He could think of nothing else. Instead of the song of the bird, however, he heard the bell of the convent ringing for service.

Felix hastened his steps; but ere he reached the convent gate, night came upon him. As he drew near the place which had been his home for many years, he did not know it— all was changed. New faces appeared at the door; strange voices chanted in the choir. Only the gray stones of spire and belfry seemed familiar to him.

"What has happened since morning, when I went into the forest to read and pray?" asked the monk of a brother who came forward to meet him. "Why are all things so changed? I see no one whom I know."

"Nearly half a century have I dwelt in this convent," replied the brother; "yet I have never seen your face before. You are a stranger here, although you wear the dress of our order."

"This morning," said Felix, who spoke as one waking from a dream, "I went alone into the forest to read and pray. In the book I read these words:

> "A thousand years in thy sight
> Are but as yesterday when it is past,
> And as a watch in the night!

"Again and again I read the words, which I believed but could not understand. Suddenly I heard the song of a bird— a snow-white bird. I followed the wondrous sound, as the bird flew from tree to tree, until I could hear it no longer. Night filled the forest with darkness. I knew no more until I heard the bell of the convent ringing for service. I hastened home, and here I am; but it seems not like home to me. Moments must have been hours!"

"Not hours, but years!" said the oldest brother of all. Then the aged man remembered that when he entered the convent, fifty years before, he was told a legend of a monk named Felix, who had gone into the forest one morning and had never returned.

"Yes," said he, looking at Felix, "this stranger must be the very man." In an old brown book, in which were kept the names of all the monks who had died, was found proof of what the aged brother said.

On a certain day, the record read, and at a certain time, one hundred years before, a monk named Felix had gone into the forest to read and pray, but had never returned. Nothing had been heard of him, and he had been counted among the dead.

"For this hundred years," exclaimed the astonished Felix, "God has given me such happiness that it has seemed but as a day!"

Felix bowed his head and prayed. He knew that while he had listened to the wondrous song of the snow-white bird in the forest, a hundred years had passed.

Thus was Felix taught the meaning of the words.

SIGURD

O thy deeds that men shall sing of;
O thy deeds that the gods shall see;
O Sigurd, Son of the Volsungs,
O victory yet to be!
~WILLIAM MORRIS —*The Story of Sigurd the Volsung*

I. THE YOUNG HERO

SIGURD was a great Northern warrior of the powerful Volsung race. His father was Sigmund, who, with his nine brothers, was taken captive by a king of the Goths and chained to an oak in the forest for the wild beasts to devour. All the Volsungs perished except Sigmund, who slew the beast that had caused the death of his brothers. Years afterward he regained his kingdom.

Sigurd's mother was the beautiful Hiordis, who, hiding in a thicket, saw her husband's sword broken at last, in a fierce battle, and that he was left to the mercy of the enemy. Hiordis rushed from her hiding place to her dying husband to hear his last message. Sigmund bade her gather the fragments of his sword, and keep them for his son, who would avenge his father's death and be a greater hero than he.

The fair Hiordis married Elf, the Viking or sea- rover, and when Sigmund's child was born he treated him like his own child, and named him Sigurd.

It was the custom in those days for the sons of a king

to be brought up and taught by a stranger, rather than at home. Sigurd was entrusted, therefore, to Regin, who was supposed to know all things— even his own fate. Sigurd learned many things from his wise teacher, not the least of which was how to be a mighty warrior.

When Sigurd grew to manhood he asked the king to give him a horse fit for battle. His request was granted at once, and he was told to choose the one he liked best of all the horses in the herd. On his way to the place where the horses were pastured, he met a one-eyed stranger, who said to him:

"Drive the horses into the river, then choose the one that breasts the waves with the greatest success."

Sigurd did so, and he noticed that one horse showed no fatigue after crossing the river, racing around the meadow on the other side, and returning again to his pasture. Sigurd selected this steed, and he called him Greyfell.

Not long after this, while the young warrior and his teacher sat together one day, Regin began to play on the harp, and to sing the story of his life, as people did in those days. This was the story that Regin sang, put into simple prose.

II. THE STORY OF REGIN

THERE was once a king of the dwarf folk (sometimes called brownies) who had three sons, Fafnir, Otter, and Regin. This king had a beautiful house, lined with gold and flashing gems, which Regin, his youngest son, had made for him, and which Fafnir, who was gifted with a powerful hand, guarded.

It chanced, once, that Odin, Hoenir, and Loki took the form of human beings and visited the earth to try the hearts of men.

They had not wandered far on the earth when they came to the place where the dwarf king dwelt. Loki saw an otter, which was the dwarf king's second son, reposing in the sun. He slew the beast, and carried the dead body over his shoulder. When Loki, with his companions, reached the house of the dwarf king, he threw the body of the otter on the floor.

As soon as the dwarf king saw what it was, he became very angry, and ordered that the three gods Odin, Hoenir, and Loki should never be freed unless they could bring him gold enough to cover the otter-skin, both inside and out. But, strange to relate, this otter-skin had the power of stretching to a wonderful size, and no small amount of treasure would cover it.

Loki, being granted his liberty in order to get the treasure, hastened to the waterfall where dwelt the dwarf Andvari, who hoarded gold by magic. He searched everywhere for Andvari; but, not finding him, he thought he must have turned into the salmon which he saw frolicking in the water.

Indeed, Loki was right, and the dwarf unwillingly brought forth his treasure, including the Helmet of Dread, and the golden coat of mail, and gave it to Loki in exchange for his freedom, keeping only the magic ring which had the power of gathering the precious metal.

But Loki was greedy, and, seeing the ring, wanted that also, and laughingly snatched it from Andvari and ran away with it. The dwarf called after him, in angry tones, that the ring thus stolen would bring sorrow and death to many.

Loki found it took all the treasure, even the magic ring, to fill the otter-skin and obtain freedom for himself and his brothers. The dwarf king was so pleased with his hoard, which Fafnir and Regin both wanted, that he watched it day and night. Fafnir, seeing he could get none of the treasure, slew his father, and put on the Helmet of Dread and the golden coat of mail. Then, when Regin came to claim his share, Fafnir drove him away with his sword, and bade him go out into the world and earn his living.

Poor Regin, who was exiled, went among men, and taught them many useful arts that they had not known— to reap and sow, sail the seas, build houses, tame horses, and spin and weave. Thus had he been waiting patiently for many years, hoping to find a hero strong enough to right the wrong his brother, Fafnir, had done, and win the treasure for him (Regin).

In the meantime, Fafnir had been changed into a horrible dragon, because he had gloated so over his stolen hoard, and had become the terror of Glittering Heath, where he dwelt. When the story was finished Regin said to Sigurd:

"Will you not slay the dragon for your old tutor?"

"I will," answered the young hero, "if you will make me a sword that nothing can break."

Regin made two swords; but when Sigurd tried them on the anvil, they broke in pieces. The brave youth, knowing he must have a sword that would not fail him, begged from his mother the broken pieces of his father's sword, which she had gathered at Sigmund's dying command. From these fragments there was such a sword made that it cut some wool floating on the river, and also broke the great anvil in two pieces, without being injured.

III. SIGURD SLAYS THE DRAGON

AFTER Sigurd had said farewell to his mother, fulfilled his promise to avenge his father's death, and reconquered his kingdom, he started with Regin to slay the dragon.

They rode over many high mountains, until at last they came to Glittering Heath, where the dragon dwelt. There they met the one-eyed stranger again, who said to Sigurd:

"Dig trenches in the path along which the dragon drags himself every day to quench his thirst at the river. Then hide in one of the trenches, and when the dragon rolls overhead, into its heart thrust your trusty sword."

Sigurd did as he was told. When the dragon rolled overhead, he thrust his sword into its heart. Then, covered with its blood, he sprang out of the trench as the monster rolled over in agony. When the sun rose again over Glittering Heath, Sigurd stood beside the dead dragon.

IV. SIGURD FINDS THE WARRIOR-MAIDEN

REGIN waited at a distance until all danger had passed, then, fearing Sigurd would glory in his deed and ask a reward, accused him of having slain his kinsman— for which he must make amends by cutting out the heart of the dragon and roasting it for him.

Sigurd, knowing it was but right, according to Northern law, to atone to the kindred of the slain, began to follow the command of Regin. In feeling of the dragon's heart to see if it were tender, he burned his fingers so severely that, without thinking, he put them in his mouth. As soon as his lips touched Fafnir's blood, Sigurd found that he could understand the songs of the birds which were gathering around from the forest. He listened and realized they were telling him what to do— to slay Regin, use the golden treasure, and eat the heart of the dragon and drink its blood.

All this Sigurd did; and putting on the Helmet of Dread, the golden coat of mail, and the magic ring, and loading Greyfell with all the gold he could carry, he rode away, the while listening to the birds as they sang to him what next to do. They sang to him of a warrior-maiden, asleep on the top of a mountain, surrounded by fire through which only the bravest of men could pass, and told him to wake her from her sleep. Sigurd rode on for miles and miles, until he came to a high mountain, the summit of which was surrounded by flames that brightened as he drew near. The young hero heard the crackle and roar of the fire; but, fearing nothing, he plunged into the midst of it. Scarcely had he done so, when the flames began to subside, leaving a circle of ashes. In the center stood a great castle, the gates of which were open and unguarded.

Sigurd, fearing all was not right, proceeded slowly to the center of the enclosure, where he beheld a form, cased in armor, motionless. He drew near and lifted the helmet, and saw, to his surprise, not a warrior, as he had supposed, but a beautiful woman asleep.

Sigurd could not waken her, however, until he had cut the armor that covered her. When he had done this, she lay before him in her white robes, with her golden hair flowing around her.

Then the beautiful maiden opened her eyes. She saw first the welcome sunlight, and then her brave deliverer, whom she loved at once.

Brunhild, for that was the maiden's name, told Sigurd that Odin, whom she served, had made her a valkyr (a battle-maiden), and that once she disobeyed him. For this disobedience Odin sent her to earth, where she must marry like any other woman. Brunhild was filled with dismay lest she should marry a coward, whom she knew she should hate. That this might not be so, Odin placed her on a mountain and "stung her with the Thorn of Sleep," that her beauty might remain unchanged. Then he surrounded her with flames, through which none but the bravest of men would dare pass. Thus was she to await the coming of her husband.

Some people say that Sigurd and the warrior-maiden parted there on the mountain; but others tell us (and we like to believe them) that they were married, and lived happily until Sigurd was forced to leave Brunhild and their little daughter. This little girl was left without father or mother when she was three years old, and was cared for by Brunhild's father.

The old man, being driven from his home, hid the child in a harp which he had made. On reaching a distant land, he was slain by some peasants for the gold they thought the harp contained.

Great was their surprise, however, when, on breaking the harp, they found a little girl, more beautiful than any they had ever seen, who would not speak a word. They kept the little one to do all their work; but when she became a maiden a powerful king of the Danes loved her and married her. Not until long after their marriage did the king know that his beautiful wife was the daughter of Sigurd, the dragon-slayer, and Brunhild, the warrior-maiden.

FRITHIOF

And then the blue-eyed Norsemen told
A Saga of the days of old.
"There is," said he, "a wondrous book
Of Legends in the old Norse tongue,
Of the dead kings of Norway,—
Legends that once were told or sung
In many a smoky fireside nook
Of Iceland in the ancient day."
~Longfellow — *Tales of a Wayside Inn*

I. FRITHIOF AND INGEBORG

THE Northmen— or Norsemen, as they are often called— spent much of their lives on the sea, which almost surrounds their land. They loved the wild life of adventure, discovery, and conquest, for which they were fitted when they were young. In the heroic days of the North, it was the custom for the eldest son to inherit his father's fortune, but the other sons were obliged to seek theirs on the ocean. Thus many of the bravest and best of those who belonged to royal families had no kingdom, and were called sea-kings. They invaded the coasts of other countries, and thought it a disgrace to return from a cruise without plunder or glory.

The Vikings, who were peasants, were the sea-rovers or pirates, and spent their time on the sea in search of plunder. They received their name from the viks, or inlets, of their land, which were the ports for their long ships.

Thorsten was one of these Vikings or sea-rovers who lived in the North. Twice he had been saved from shipwreck by an old witch, whom he promised to marry because she had saved his life. Now the old witch was really a beautiful young girl, named Ingeborg, the daughter of a king. Her father had been killed by an enemy, her brother had been sent out of the country, and she had been changed into the form of an old witch.

Ingeborg urged Thorsten to find her brother, Belé, as he was called, and restore to him the kingdom which was his by right. This the Viking did, and he and Belé promised to be friends ever after. At once the old witch was changed again into the beautiful young girl, and Thorsten married her, as he promised when she saved him from drowning.

This couple had only one child, named Frithiof (the peacemaker), who became one of the most fearless as well as the most famous Vikings of the North. His story has been told and sung in almost every language, and in the Northern countries it is cherished alike by rich and poor.

King Belé had three children — two sons, named Helgé and Halfdan, and one little daughter, named Ingeborg. All were companions of Frithiof, the bonder's (farmer's) child. But Ingeborg was especially entrusted to the care of old Hilding,

Frithiof's foster-father. So the boy and girl were together day after day. Frithiof and Ingeborg grew in strength and beauty, even as their love did. When the lad went hunting and brought home his first bear, he laid it at his playmate's feet.

During the long evenings of the Northern winter, Frithiof read, by the light of the burning logs, wondrous tales of devotion, adventure, and conquest— of Odin, Thor, and Frey (from whom we get the names Wednesday, Thursday, and Friday), of heroes and valkyrs. The valkyrs were beautiful battle-maidens, who watched over the battle-fields and bore away the heroes that were slain, or over the sea and rescued the Vikings from their sinking ships. But no maiden, thought Frithiof, no matter how brave or how fair, could compare with Ingeborg, with her white skin, her golden hair, and her blue eyes.

Ingeborg, as she sat at her loom day after day, sang the

stories of heroes, and wove them into the tapestry before her. Strange to say, the hero of the story always grew more and more like Frithiof. But no hero, thought Ingeborg, could be too brave or too noble to bear the likeness of her playfellow.

With sadness did old Hilding, their foster-father, notice that the children were happiest when they were together. He knew it could not last long, for you remember that Ingeborg was the daughter of a king, while poor Frithiof was only the subject of a king. When the old man spoke to Frithiof of this growing love for his little companion, and tried to show him, before it was too late, that no good could come of it, the boy laughingly shouted:

"It is too late already! I shall win the fair Ingeborg for my bride, in spite of every one— even great Thor, the Thunderer! Nothing shall part us!"

In the spring, when the ice had melted enough to let their great ships pass, King Belé and Thorsten set sail to recover lost treasures from distant lands. This they had done for many, many years. Now they had grown old and feeble. They felt they no longer had the strength of youth to guide the mighty ships on dangerous voyages. There was to be no more spring for them— nothing but winter. The time had come for them to go on a long journey from which they would never return.

So the old warriors called their heirs together, near the shrine of Balder. Balder was thought by the Norsemen to bring the sunshine to the earth, and on the longest day in the year, the middle of the Northern summer, they had a great festival and made bonfires in honor of Balder, the good and beautiful. There it was the old men spoke to their children for the last time.

King Belé told Helgé and Halfdan that his time was short. He wished them to love Frithiof as he and Thorsten had loved each other. He bade them to keep peace, if possible, and use their swords only to protect themselves and their kingdom.

Then Thorsten spoke to Frithiof, who was the tallest and the fairest of the three. He bade him do right and shun evil, envying no one who was above him.

At last the old friends told of their long friendship, which had lasted through peace and war. This they gave now to their children, bidding them cherish it as a priceless gift. King Belé finished his speech by sending a greeting to his daughter, Ingeborg, and begged Helgé to care for her as a father, and to guard her from all harm. He then added:

"My old friend and I are on our way to the place of rest, for which we both long. Lay us in two mounds, in sight of each other, beside the water. Go you back to your busy life again, my children. The blessings of the mighty ones go with you. Farewell!"

II. THE SWORD, THE RING, AND THE SHIP

THE king and his faithful subject and friend were laid in the mounds by the side of the water, as they had desired. Helgé and Halfdan ruled the kingdom together.

Frithiof received three priceless gifts from his father,

which he prized greatly. The first was a wondrous sword that had been made by the dwarfs and owned by heroes. It was famous throughout all the North. The second gift was a magic ring of gold, on which were graven many scenes and stories dear to the Norsemen. Once this ring had been stolen by a pirate or sea-robber. He was so afraid someone would get his treasure that he buried himself alive with it in a mound, where he watched it day and night.

When King Belé and Thorsten went on one of their yearly voyages which you have just read about, they sought the place where the pirate and the ring were hidden. After many difficulties, Thorsten entered the mound and recovered the ring, which had come to him from his mother, and was of great value.

The third gift was the good ship Ellida, which the ruler of the sea and father of the waves and winds had given to Thorsten's father, because he was kind to a poor shipwrecked stranger.

> A royal gift to behold, for the swelling planks of its framework
> Were not fastened with nails, as is wont, but grown in together.
> Its shape was that of a dragon, when swimming, but forward
> Its head rose proudly on high, the throat with yellow gold flaming.
> ~Tegnér — *Frithiof Saga* (Spalding's Tr.)

So you see that although he had no crown or kingdom, Frithiof owned the three greatest gifts in all the North—the sword, the ring, and the ship.

Frithiof had a dear friend and companion named Bjorn, whom he had known and loved from childhood. The two boys had promised to share good and evil fortune together, like Roland and Oliver, and to defend each other if need be.

Frithiof lived in his beautiful home, which his father had given him besides the three gifts already mentioned. When the long winter was over, and the welcome spring had come, Frithiof's heart rejoiced; for King Helgé and King Halfdan brought their little sister Ingeborg to visit him in his beautiful but lonely home. It was then that Frithiof and Ingeborg lived over the happy days when they were children. Many were the pleasant hours they spent talking to each other as they roamed through the meadows.

Ingeborg whispered gently to her companion that she was much happier with him than in the royal castle, and then added:

"Of all the doves we raised together, only one pair is left. You take one, and I the other. If you ever tie a message under its wing, it will fly to its mate at once."

Like the Northern spring, the happy days were soon over. The guests returned to their home. Again Frithiof was lonely and sad. He sent a message by the dove, as Ingeborg had told him, but he received no reply to his message, for the bird would not leave its mate.

Bjorn saw with dismay that his friend was growing more and more downhearted every day. Something must be done, he thought; but what?

It was not long, however, before Frithiof told his friend that he must see Ingeborg and ask her brothers to give her to him for his wife. So the great ship Ellida was made ready for the voyage, and Frithiof guided it toward Ingeborg's home.

III. ONLY THE SUBJECT OF A KING

In a short time Frithiof stood before the two kings and asked them for their sister. He told them how he loved her; how their father, the king, had always loved him; how he had allowed them to be brought up by the same foster-father. Then Frithiof promised if they would grant his request that he would serve them with his right arm whenever it was needed.

When King Helgé heard Frithiof's words he was very angry, and replied:

"Our sister is of royal blood— the daughter of a king. You are only a king's subject. No, it cannot be."

If King Helgé was angry, Frithiof was more so. He struck the royal shield, which hung on a tree near by, with his sword, and turned in silence and dismay toward his ship Ellida.

There was an old king in Norway named Ring. He had a beautiful wife, and when she died he thought to ask Ingeborg to take her place and be his queen. So he sent a number of attendants, bearing precious and costly gifts to King Helgé's court. There they were royally entertained for three days.

King Helgé tried to find in many different ways (as people did in those days) if it would be well for his sister to marry King Ring. As all the signs were unfavorable to the marriage, he bade the messengers depart and tell the old king it could not be.

When King Ring heard the answer, however, he was very angry. He called his people together, and bade them prepare to march against these kings, who had insulted him thus.

Now you must know that King Helgé was a great coward. When he heard that the powerful King Ring was coming, he was afraid. So he did just what cowards generally do: he sought for some one else to meet the danger for him — he sent Hilding to Frithiof, whom he had treated so unkindly, to ask him to come and help them. In the meantime, Ingeborg was hidden in Balder's temple, where she was thought to be safe from all harm.

Hilding did as his king had asked him; but he went with a fearful heart. He found Frithiof and Bjorn playing a game of chess, in which they were very much interested. Frithiof joyfully welcomed his foster-father, whom he was delighted to see until he heard the reason for his visit.

Frithiof had been so offended by King Helgé, that he paid no attention to the messages and entreaties brought by Hilding, but kept on with his game of chess. At last, Hilding, growing tired and fearing the result of this silence, exclaimed in despair:

"Ingeborg is kept a prisoner in Balder's temple, where she sits weeping all day at her work. Will you not come for her sake?"

At this Frithiof rose quickly, and told Hilding there was no answer for the kings who had just refused his help when he offered it. Hilding was obliged to return without an answer. The kings, not being able or willing to meet the enemy without Frithiof, made an agreement with King Ring, promising to give him not only their sister but a sum of money every year as well.

As soon as Frithiof heard from Hilding where Ingeborg

was hidden, he decided to see her once more in spite of all danger. This he confided to Bjorn, to whom he told everything, and his faithful friend promised to go with him to Balder's temple. The dragon-ship was made ready, and after a short voyage reached the shore where the temple stood.

Then it was that Frithiof and Ingeborg told each other again of their love and loneliness. Frithiof gave Ingeborg the magic ring, which she promised to send to him when she cared for him no longer.

After Frithiof had seen Ingeborg and knew her distress, he was sorry he had refused to help the kings. In spite of his great pride, again he appeared before them, and again offered his right arm to defend their kingdom if they would give him their sister for his wife.

All the warriors who stood listening to the noble youth were rejoiced, and begged that his wish might be granted. Hilding, and even Halfdan, pleaded for it also; but still King Helgé refused. He asked Frithiof if he had not talked with Ingeborg in the temple. If so, he had broken the law, for which he must be punished. The people hoped Frithiof could say no to this question, but Frithiof told the truth, although he knew his happiness would be lost by doing so. He replied that he had talked with Ingeborg at Balder's shrine— then waited in silence to hear his punishment.

In great anger, King Helgé cried:

"The law of our fathers for such a deed as this is either exile or death; but I shall punish you another way. There is a group of islands [the Orkneys], far away in the West, over which an earl rules. Every year he used to bring tribute to my father; but he has never done so since my father's death. If you can get this tribute that is due and bring it to me, your life shall be spared."

With breaking heart Frithiof hastened to Ingeborg and told her of the task that had been given him by her brother. He then begged her to go with him (when he should have redeemed his word and brought the tribute) in the good ship Ellida to the sunny South. There they might make a happy home for themselves.

Poor Ingeborg, amid sobs and tears, told him she could not go against the command of her brother, although she knew in obeying him her happiness would be lost.

After a sorrowful parting, Frithiof sailed away in his dragon-ship. Ingeborg wept as she stood sadly watching the sails of the mighty vessel as it disappeared from sight.

IV. A VOYAGE FOR GOLD

No sooner had the Viking set sail than King Helgé sent for two witches to stir up a terrible storm. It was so violent that even the magic ship Ellida was powerless against it. Frithiof kept a brave heart until the waves rose so high and the winds blew so fiercely that he feared all was lost. Bidding Bjorn take the helm, he climbed to the very topmast that he might see as far as possible. What do you think he saw? A great whale with two witches riding on its back, and stirring up the storm that bid fair to wreck the ship!

Frithiof called upon his good ship Ellida (for it was said

that Ellida understood her master's words) and begged her to overcome the witches and save him and his crew. Instantly the magic ship plunged right in the direction of the whale, and struck it. Both the monster and the witches, being mortally hurt, sank beneath the waves.

At once the wind ceased, the sea became calm, and the welcome sun rose high in the heavens. Frithiof was filled with joy, and he and his men drank a health to fair Ingeborg.

The watchmen in the earl's palace saw the great ship in the distance. At once they knew it was Ellida bringing Thorsten's son. One of the earl's champions made ready to fight the Viking as soon as he should land.

Although Frithiof, after the perilous voyage, was weary, he did not hesitate to meet the enemy.

So fierce and long was the struggle that the friends looked on with fear, lest one or the other might be slain. At length Frithiof was acknowledged the victor, and the wrestlers walked side by side to the feast which had been awaiting them. In a friendly way, they ate and drank, and told of strange adventures on both land and sea. The earl spoke words of welcome to Frithiof and in loving remembrance of his old friend Thorsten. While they feasted and made merry, the sweet notes of the harp were heard. The minstrel sang songs in praise of Thorsten, the famous Viking of the North.

Finally, Frithiof told the earl of his dangerous voyage, of Ingeborg, and of King Helgé who had sent him to claim the tribute of gold.

When the earl heard this he exclaimed:

"I pay no tribute to King Helgé, neither shall I; but here

is gold for you, son of my old friend, for a welcome. Do with it what you will."

The earl begged Frithiof to spend the winter with him, and was pleased when he promised to do so. It was not until the spring had come and the time for the fierce storms had passed that Frithiof sailed for home.

After a voyage of six days he neared the land, when, alas! he beheld nothing but ruins and ashes. As soon as Frithiof landed he sought old Hilding, of whom he asked with fear:

"Where is Ingeborg?"

Poor Hilding, who seemed to be the one whose task it was to answer all the hard questions, was almost afraid to tell Frithiof all that had happened since Ellida had borne him away. But, knowing that someone must tell the anxious Viking the truth, he did so with much hesitation. Hilding told him how King Ring came with a mighty army, and would accept no terms of peace unless Ingeborg would be his wife. Then Hilding paused a minute, and Frithiof, thinking Ingeborg had forgotten him, burst forth in wild exclamations.

"Not so," cried Hilding, quickly; "her suffering is greater than any one knows. Her life is a misery. On her wedding day I lifted her in my own arms from the saddle, and she whispered to me of her unhappiness. King Helgé, seeing the ring that you had given her on her arm, snatched it from her roughly."

Frithiof could bear no more. He ordered all the vessels in the harbor to be destroyed, and bade Bjorn keep watch at the gate. Then he went in search of King Helgé, whom he found in the temple, standing before the image of Balder.

As soon as the angry youth beheld his enemy, he flung the purse of gold which, you remember, the earl had given him into King Helgé's face.

Catching sight of the magic ring on the arm of the statue, Frithiof seized it violently. In doing so, the statue fell into the fire beneath. The flames rose quickly and set the roof on fire. Every one was filled with horror and dismay. Frithiof, overcome by what he had done unwittingly, tried to put out the fire.

When he found he could do no more, he fled to his ship, broken-hearted.

But King Helgé was not willing that Frithiof should escape unharmed. So he made one more effort to destroy him. As the magic ship sailed out of the harbor with her master on board, she was met by ten of the king's finest vessels, sent to capture Frithiof.

Again King Helgé was thwarted in his plans. Secretly and silently, Bjorn had bored a hole in the bottom of each vessel, and one by one they sank beneath the waves. The king was the only one who escaped.

As Ellida steered for the open sea, Frithiof bade farewell to all he loved best, expecting never to return. He became a great sea-rover or pirate. His deeds were known and talked about in many lands. He had his men make no place their home, sleep on their shields, and fight the ships that did not pay him tribute. The goods they captured he divided among them, he being content with the glory of conquest.

So Frithiof, the Viking, visited many countries and sailed many seas, fighting and capturing. At last he reached the sunny land of Greece, where he had hoped once to take Ingeborg and make their home.

Again his thoughts were of her— of his native land, the North, where she was sad and lonely.

"Three years have passed," he cried, "since I left my native land, my beloved country — all that I love best. I must go back. I must see Ingeborg once more!"

So saying, the Viking steered his good ship for the North.

V. A BEGGAR AT THE KING's FEAST

LEAVING his ship in Bjorn's care and disguising himself as a beggar, the Viking made his way to the court of King Ring. It was the Christmas time. The aged king and the young queen were seated at the feast, when an unknown beggar entered, and seated himself near the door. Some of the company began making fun of him. One of their number carried his fun a little too far, and the next instant he was tossed high in the air by the unbidden guest. King Ring, hearing the noise, invited the beggar to throw off his cloak and hood, and draw near and tell him his name, his country, and his errand at court.

As the stranger drew near, the ragged mantle fell from his head and shoulders. To the surprise and wonder of all present, there stood a noble youth, with high brow, and golden locks that fell on his broad, manly shoulders. His arms were covered with bands of gold, and by his side hung a glistening sword— a hero stood before the king and queen, in the midst of the Christmas festival.

Immediately the queen knew it was Frithiof; but she made no sign of it, save by the flush on her fair cheeks. In vain did the king question the guest as to his story, until the sound of the horn was heard— a signal that the hour for taking vows for the new year had come.

King Ring vowed to capture Frithiof, the bold Viking, whose fame had become known throughout the land. The stranger vowed to defend him with his trusty sword.

The minstrel sang of adventure and war and devotion, to the sweet notes of the harp. All went merrily at the Christmas feast.

VI. A NOBLE YOUTH

King Ring begged the stranger to remain at court and be his companion wherever he went.

"Is it right for me to stay?" Frithiof asked himself; "yet the queen gives no sign that she knows me." The old king, however, would not listen to any other arrangement, and as time went on he grew more and more fond of the noble youth who had come unbidden and unwelcomed to the feast.

Once when the king and queen were sleighing, and Frithiof was racing ahead of them on his skates carving Ingeborg's name, the ice gave way, and king, queen, and sleigh plunged beneath it into the water. Instantly, Frithiof jumped in after them, and carried them in his strong arms to a place of safety.

Another time, Frithiof went on a hunting expedition

with them. The king, being weary, was not able to keep up with the rest of the party, and sought a place of rest. His young companion remained by his side, spread his mantle on the ground, and the old king rested his head on Frithiof's knees and slept.

It will be remembered, perhaps, how Sigurd, another hero of the North, understood the birds when they sang to him in the forest. So it was with Frithiof. He listened; and it was the black bird calling to him:

"Now is your time to strike and take your bride away. No one can see or hear!"

As the last note died away, another sound was heard. It was the white bird calling to him:

"Harm not the old man, for he is unarmed. Odin will see and hear!"

Frithiof listened, and obeyed the call of the white bird. He flung his sword into the thicket near by, lest he should be too sorely tempted to harm his feeble host.

It was not long before King Ring awoke. Indeed, you may as well know he had not been asleep. He only pretended to be so, that he might test Frithiof, whom he had known from the first. Now he was satisfied, for he had tried him in every way, and found him most worthy and honorable.

The old king knew he could not live much longer; but while he lived he wanted Frithiof to be like his own son. This he told to the young man, and added:

"When I am dead, take my queen, my little son, and my kingdom. I leave them all in your care."

Frithiof was overcome at the words he heard. Silently

he led the old man home. When they reached there, King Ring laid the queen's hand in the hand of the Viking, and he spoke no more.

VII. THE VIKING'S REWARD

AFTER King Ring had been laid at rest, the people assembled to elect a new king. Frithiof, brave and fair, stood in the midst of the nobles. By his side stood the golden-haired son of King Ring. Frithiof, raising the child on his shield, that all the people might see him, proclaimed him their new king. He promised to guide and help the little one until he should be old enough to rule alone. The lad, wearied with his position on the shield, jumped to the ground while Frithiof was still speaking. This delighted the people, who shouted and hailed both Frithiof and the child with encouraging words.

Frithiof hastened at once to the mound by the water, where his father was buried. Then he visited Balder's shrine, where he beheld a vision of a new temple, grand and beautiful. From this vision he knew he was to rebuild the temple which, unwittingly, he had destroyed.

When the new temple was finished, Frithiof laid his sword and dagger on the altar as a sign of peace. As he did so, the fair Ingeborg, dressed in her wedding gown, was led by her brother to the altar, where she gave her hand to the noble Viking.

WILLIAM TELL

A STATUE OF WILLIAM TELL AT ALTDORF

Switzerland is a small but very beautiful country, with snow-capped mountains, deep valleys, and picturesque lakes. Its people are strong, proud, and brave, and very fond of their country. The peasants spend much of their time in caring for the flocks and herds, or hunting the wild chamois or goat that dwells among the ice cliffs of the Alps. The skins of these little animals are so valuable that a hunter often risks his life in pursuing them from cliff to cliff. The Swiss love to tell the story of their hero, William Tell, who, it is said, made his country free.

Many hundred years ago, Switzerland was conquered and ruled by strangers from across the mountains, who sent a man named Gessler to rule the people.

This man was a cruel tyrant who ruled unjustly—in fact, he made slaves of the Swiss. He built many fortresses throughout the country, and filled them with soldiers in order to frighten the proud people into submission. But even then he could not make them bow down to him as he wished. This made him angry, and he thought of another way to torment them. He set up a pole in the marketplace, where the peasants came to sell their game, butter, and cheese, and buy what they needed for their mountain homes. On the pole Gessler placed his hat as a sign of his power. Then he commanded that every Swiss man, woman, and child who passed by the pole should bow to the hat to show their respect for him. The people had been growing more and more indignant at the way their rights were being taken from them, and were eager and ready to find some way of gaining their freedom.

One night, not long after this, William Tell returned to his mountain home, near Altorf, very sad and unhappy. His wife, knowing there was something the matter, said:

"There is sadness in your voice and trouble in your face. Will you not trust me with the cause of it?"

"You know, my loving wife," said Tell, "the sad state of slavery to which this unhappy country of Switzerland is reduced by the unjust oppression of our foreign rulers."

"Yes," replied his wife; "but what have peasants to do with these matters?"

"Much, indeed!" answered Tell; "if the good laws made for the comfort and protection of all ranks of people, all the old customs which were the pride and glory of our land, are set aside by strangers, then it is the duty of peasants as well as nobles to defend their rights. I have joined myself with thirty-three of my countrymen to find a way to free our land."

"It would be impossible for thirty-three men to oppose the power that rules Switzerland," said Tell's wife, turning pale at the thought. "Gessler cares nothing for what peasants think. What has he done now?"

"He has found a way to tell the freeman from the slave throughout the country, by erecting a pole in the marketplace, on which he has placed his hat, and commanded every Swiss man, woman, and child to bow before it, or meet their death. Do you think I would stoop to such a thing, and bear the name of Swiss?" said Tell.

"No," answered his wife; "I know you will never submit to that. But do not go to Altorf, my husband."

"My business calls me there," Tell replied; "whither I shall go like an honest man and do my duty. I shall be neither a slave nor a coward, my good wife."

There was a fair held at Altorf, where men went from all the country round to sell their goods.

William Tell had risen early that morning, and had gone there to sell his chamois-skins and make some purchases for his wife and children. He had taken with him his little son, and together they crossed the marketplace and stood directly opposite the spot where the pole had been erected. Tell never bent his head, but stood as proud and as straight as ever. The soldiers who had been stationed there by Gessler to make the people obey, stopped the bold hunter of the mountains and reminded him of the punishment for not showing respect to the hat.

Gessler's spies, who had been watching Tell, told the tyrant of his defiance. At once he commanded the Swiss to be brought before him, and he came, leading his little son by the hand.

"You are a skillful archer, they tell me," said the tyrant; "the most skillful in all this country. You shall give me proof of this wonderful skill, and thus have one chance of saving your life, which you forfeited by disobeying my command. No doubt your boy is made of the same stuff as you are. Let him stand a hundred paces, yonder. Then place an apple on his head, and if you can shoot an arrow so truly as to cut the apple in two, your life is spared. But if you either slay the child or miss the apple, you lose your life instantly."

"Cruel tyrant," cried the distracted father, as he drew two

arrows from his quiver, "do you think I would try to save my own life by risking that of my child?"

"You shall either shoot the arrow or die!" replied Gessler; "it is my command."

"My choice is already made," said Tell, letting the bow fall from his hands; "let me die!"

"But the child shall be slain before your eyes, traitor, if you will not shoot at him."

In despair, Tell asked for his bow once more.

Then two servants of Gessler led the lad away a hundred paces, and placed an apple on his head. They had some pity left in their hearts for the father, and so, as he had requested, they made the boy stand with his back to him.

A great crowd had gathered around the linden tree, beneath which the child was bound. The people turned pale with fear, as Tell's lips moved in prayer, and the dreadful silence was broken by the archer's clear voice, as it rang out:

"Face this way, my boy."

The child turned instantly, and faced his father, his arms hanging straight and motionless, his head erect. He saw his father try his bow to see if it were true, and bring the bowstring into place — then he shut his eyes.

The awful stillness was broken once more— this time by the sharp twang of the bowstring, answered by a shout from the crowd:

"The arrow has cut the apple in two— the boy is safe!"

"It is well!" exclaimed the brave archer, on whom the applause from the crowd for his successful shot had fallen unheeded. But before the grateful father could take his child in his arms, the cruel Gessler demanded for what purpose he had selected two arrows, having seen him place the second one in his belt. "That arrow was for you, tyrant," said Tell, in a burst of anger, "had I missed my first shot."

"You have spoken frankly," said Gessler. "I have promised you your life. I will not break my word; but I shall place you in a dungeon, where you shall see neither sun nor moon, and your arrow shall do no more harm." Then he commanded the soldiers to seize Tell, and place him on board a small vessel, and when they had reached a certain spot to put him in a dungeon there for life.

The famous bow, with the quiver and arrows, was placed for safety at the feet of the master-pilot. The vessel had only fairly started when a terrible storm arose. The wicked Gessler, like most wicked people, was afraid. He and all his crew were in danger of being lost, when one of his men reminded him that William Tell was as skillful in the management of a boat as in the use of the bow.

So the frightened Gessler ordered that Tell should be unbound, and placed at the helm. The boat, steered by the unfailing hand of the fearless Tell, kept its steady course in the midst of the storm. Just as the vessel was turned toward the land, Tell noticed a high rock, and called to the rowers to row with all their might till they should have passed the danger ahead. At the very instant they reached this point, the swift-footed archer snatched his bow, which had been forgotten during the storm, sprang on shore, scaled the mountain, and was out of sight before anyone had time to know what had happened.

Tell hid himself in a thicket on the road along which Gessler would pass on the way to his castle, if he reached land in safety. When Gessler and his men did pass the spot where Tell was hiding, he heard the merciless tyrant exclaim:

"When I return to Altorf, I shall destroy that traitor Tell, his wife, and his children in the same hour."

"You shall never return to Altorf!" whispered Tell, fitting an arrow to his faithful bow. The arrow went as truly and as surely as the one he had shot in the market-place of Altorf. The tyrant Gessler fell from his horse as a familiar voice shouted:

"My brave uncle, that was a well-aimed shot! Gessler is slain, and we are free." It was the voice of Tell's young nephew, who had come to tell his uncle that his countrymen were waiting for him, if he could only make his escape.

In the darkness of night Tell and his nephew reached the town, where they met the little band of patriots who had joined themselves together to defend their rights and free their beloved country from the foreign yoke. They received their hero with open arms. In a few days the whole country was roused, and ready to fight. The forces of the emperor were defeated everywhere by the brave, hardy patriots, and Switzerland was free.

And William Tell, the fearless hunter, lived happily with his family in his mountain home, surrounded by his countrymen, with whom he had fought for the freedom of Switzerland.

THE BELL OF ATRI

.... Your story pleads the cause
Of those dumb mouths that have no speech.
~LONGFELLOW— *Tales of a Wayside Inn*

In the olden times there was a good king who had a great bell hung in the marketplace of the town of Atri. It was covered by a roof, which sheltered it from sun and rain. When the bell was in place, the king rode through the streets, and proclaimed, with loud trumpets, that if wrong was done to any man he should ring this bell and justice would be given him.

For a long time all went well in the little town of Atri. Many wrongs were made right by the ringing of the great bell that hung in the public square.

After a while the rope that hung from the bell became worn, and the strands at the end were unraveled. Someone, passing by, noticed the worn-out end and mended it with a vine, the leaves of which hung over the loosened strands.

At that time there lived in Atri a knight who, in his youth, had loved all sorts of outdoor sports. He had loved his horses, his falcons, and his dogs. But when he became too old to enjoy all these things that once had given him so much pleasure, he cared for nothing but getting and saving money. He sold all his horses, his hawks, and his hounds, and rented all his vineyards and his gardens in order to get more gold. He kept only one poor old horse, his favorite of all, and let him shiver and starve in a bare stall.

Day after day, the wretched, unhappy knight thought and planned how to spend less and save more.

Finally, he thought of the one horse he had left, and he said to himself:

"Why need I keep that lazy old steed to eat his head off? Rents are low, and food is high. I shall let him feed by the roadside, for I shall need him only on holidays."

So the old horse, that had served his master long and well, was turned into the street, and allowed to wander from place to place, hungry and forlorn.

On a sudden, one day, the great bell in the marketplace roused the people of Atri from their sleep. The magistrate, or officer of the law, hurried to the place to see what had happened that the bell should be rung. As he drew near the belfry he heard the old song as it seemed to say:

Someone hath done a wrong, hath done a wrong!

As he drew near, he saw neither man nor woman, but a poor old horse pulling eagerly at the leaves that covered the end of the rope, and he cried:

"This is the knight of Atri's horse that calls thus for justice, and asks for help, in his own way."

Suddenly a great crowd gathered, and heard the story, which was told in different ways by one and another. When the knight was sent for and questioned about the matter, he treated it as a jest, and said he should do as he pleased with his own.

Then the magistrate read what the king had said when the bell was hung in the market-place, and added:

> "Pride goeth forth on horseback grand and gay,
> But Cometh back on foot, and begs its way;
> Fame is the fragrance of heroic deeds,
> Of flowers of chivalry and not of weeds!"
> ~LONGFELLOW— *The Bell of Atri*

He asked the knight what good could come to him for starving a poor horse that was unable to make his wants known; and said that since the animal had served him well in his youth, he must provide food and shelter for him in his old age.

The knight was ashamed, and went away. The people led the poor old horse back to his master's stable.

When the king heard the story he was greatly pleased. He declared that the Bell of Atri, since it could right the wrongs of dumb creatures and give them relief, should be made famous in all lands forever.

KING ROBERT OF SICILY

King Robert of Sicily was such a proud man that he thought no one in the world was as powerful and as great as he. Once, when he sat in church, thinking of himself and all he possessed, he heard these words chanted:

> He has put down the mighty from their seat,
> And has exalted them of low degree.
> ~Longfellow— *King Robert of Sicily*

This made the proud king very angry, and he said to himself that no power could push him from his throne. As the words were repeated again and again to the low, unvaried music, he fell asleep.

It was night when King Robert awoke and found himself alone. The church was dark, except for a few flickering lights here and there. He groped his way to the door, but it was locked securely. Then he knocked and cried aloud for some one to come to him. But when he listened he heard only the sound he had made as it echoed through the solitary place.

At length the sexton, hearing the unusual noise, thought there must be thieves in the church. So, taking his lantern to guide him, he called from without and asked who was there.

In angry tones the king replied:

"'T is I, the king."

As the frightened sexton opened the door, out rushed

a wild-looking creature, without hat or cloak, who neither spoke nor turned as he fled into the darkness.

King Robert, without his magnificent robes, bareheaded and out of breath, reached the palace gate. In shame he hurried past guards and pages, and up the broad stairway. From room to room he went in haste, until he reached the banquet hall, which was ablaze with light and filled with guests.

To King Robert's horror and dismay, he saw *another* king, but with his face and form, wearing his crown, his robes, his ring, and seated on his throne. He could neither speak nor move. As he gazed in helpless silence, the angel king (for such he was) asked gently:

"Who are you? and why do you come here?"

With impatience and anger, King Robert answered: *"I am the king*, and have come to take only that which is mine."

At these words the angry guests arose and drew their swords, but the angel said calmly:

"No, you are not the king, but the king's jester. Hereafter you shall wear the cap and bells such as jesters wear, and, led by an ape, shall obey my servants when they call."

The poor king's cries and threats were unheeded as he was thrust from the banquet hall, while courtiers and pages mocked him and laughingly shouted:

"Long live the king!"

The next morning, King Robert wakened with the first ray of light. He said to himself he was happy that it was all a dream, and that he was himself again. But when he moved he felt the coarse straw rustle; he saw the cap and bells, and in the corner the shivering, hideous ape. No dream indeed! He thought the world he loved so well had turned to dust.

The angel ruled the happy island well, while the poor jester thought, in silence, of the change that had brought him so low. Still he was as proud as ever, and would not bend his head. When the angel met him and asked tenderly if he were the king still, he raised his head as proudly as before, and answered:

"I AM — I AM THE KING!"

After three years had passed, King Robert was sent for by his brother to come to Rome. The angel received the messengers with joy, and gave them precious gifts. Then he came with them to Rome, where he was welcomed with shouts of joy and the sound of trumpets.

In the gay procession of riders, with their jeweled bridles and their golden spurs, rode the poor jester, with the ape, and amused the people of the towns through which they passed. Just as the angel was receiving great honors, suddenly there was a stir among the crowd, through which the jester rushed to his brother and cried piteously:

> "I am the King! Look, and behold in me
> Robert, your brother, King of Sicily!"
> ~LONGFELLOW— *King Robert of Sicily*

His brother looked at the strange creature, in cap and bells, and wondered that such a madman should be kept at court. The unhappy jester was hurried back to his place amid the jeers and shouts of the people.

When Easter Sunday came, the presence of the angel

filled the city with light, and the hearts of men with kindness and love. Even the jester felt a power, unknown before, as he knelt humbly on his bare floor and raised his eyes to see the splendor of the light.

When the visit was ended, the angel returned to Sicily and ruled the island as before. One evening, as he heard the bell for church, he beckoned to the jester to draw near, and bade the others leave them alone. Then he asked gently:

"Are you still the king?"

Meekly, King Robert bowed his head and answered:

"You know best. Let me go and ask to be forgiven for my pride of wealth and power."

The angel smiled. A great light filled the hall. King Robert listened, and in the distance he heard the same words he had heard when he fell asleep in the church:

> He hath put down the mighty from their seat,
> And has exalted them of low degree!

As he listened to the familiar words, he seemed to hear another voice that said:

"I am an angel, and you are the king. I have watched over your kingdom, which I now give back to you. You were proud, but now you are humble and able to rule."

King Robert raised his head, and, lo! he was alone, dressed in his robes of ermine and cloth of gold, as of old.

And when the courtiers came, they found King Robert kneeling on the floor in silent prayer.

THE PIED PIPER OF HAMELIN

A very long time ago, the town of Hamelin was over run with rats. The people had no peace, and they did not know what to do to get rid of them. We are told there were so many rats that—

> They fought the dogs and killed the cats,
>   And bit the babies in the cradles,
> And ate the cheeses out of the vats,
>   And licked the soup from the cooks' own ladles,
> Split open the kegs of salted sprats,
> Made nests inside men's Sunday hats,
> And even spoiled the women's chats,
>   By drowning their speaking
>   With shrieking and squeaking
> In fifty different sharps and flats.
>   ~Robert Browning — *The Pied Piper of Hamelin*

The trouble grew worse every day. At last the people could bear it no longer. So they went to the town hall, where the mayor and the townsmen were assembled. They asked them if something could not be done to rid the town of the terrible torments.

For more than an hour the mayor sat silent, puzzling his brain what to do. He had just begun to speak, when, hearing a knock at the door, he called loudly for the intruder to come in.

In the doorway stood a queer-looking creature, dressed in a long coat, half yellow and half red. Around his neck was a scarf, also of yellow and red, from which hung a curious pipe.

To the surprise of all present, the stranger walked toward the mayor, and said that he was able to draw all creatures, of every description, to him by a secret charm. Then he told that he was called the Pied Piper, which means he was dressed in different colors, such as a jester or clown wears, and that he had done wonderful things with his magic music.

The strange piper, having heard how the town was beset with rats, offered to drive them all away, so they would never return, if the people would give him a certain sum of money.

The mayor and townsmen were relieved to find some one to help them out of the difficulty. They willingly promised the poor piper more than the sum he asked for his trouble.

Into the street went the piper, and putting the pipe to his lips, he blew a few shrill notes. No sooner had he done so, than a great grumbling was heard from all directions:

> And the grumbling grew to a mighty rumbling,
> And out of the houses the rats came tumbling;
> Great rats, small rats, lean rats, brawny rats,
> Brown rats, black rats, grey rats, tawny rats,
> Grave old plodders, gay young friskers,
> Fathers, mothers, uncles, cousins,
> Cocking tails, and pricking whiskers,
> Families by tens and dozens;
> Brothers, sisters, husbands, wives —
> Followed the Piper for their lives.
> ~Robert Browning— *The Pied Piper of Hamelin*

On went the rats, following the music of the piper, until they reached the river, into which they all plunged, and were drowned— save one fat old rat that swam to the other side, and lived to tell the story of the piper's call.

The people of Hamelin were so overjoyed to be rid of the torments that they rang the bells of the churches. The mayor ordered that no trace of the rats should be left in the town.

But what of the poor piper who had done it all? When he appeared in the marketplace, and asked, "My money, if you please?" the mayor and people, thinking the rats could never return to trouble them more, were sorry they had made such a bargain with the piper, and refused to pay him. They laughed, and pretending it was all a joke, offered him a small part of what they had promised to pay.

At this the piper grew angry. He told them if they kept him waiting much longer for his money, he would pipe for them in another way.

The mayor, not wishing to give up the money, paid no attention to the piper's threats; but told him to do his worst— never dreaming what his worst might be.

THE HOUSE OF THE PIED PIPER

Into the street went the piper, and putting the pipe to his lips, he blew a few sweet notes. No sooner had he done so than a rustling was heard from all directions:

> There was a rustling that seemed like a bustling
> Of merry crowds justling at pitching and hustling,
> Small feet were pattering, wooden shoes clattering,
> Little hands clapping and little tongues chattering,
> And, like fowls in a farmyard when barley is scattering,
> Out came the children running.
> ~Robert Browning — *The Pied Piper of Hamelin*

The boys and girls, with rosy cheeks and bright eyes, shouted, laughed, and danced as they followed the magic music of the piper. The mayor and the people stood dumb and helpless. At last, with a sigh of relief, they saw the piper and the gay procession turn toward a high hill, and they cried:

> "He never can cross that mighty top!
> He's forced to let the piping drop,
> And we shall see our children stop!"
> ~Robert Browning— *The Pied Piper of Hamelin*

But before they had time to finish, the mountain opened like a great door, and closed again when all the little ones were inside. No, not all; for one little lame fellow, who was not able to dance all the way, was left just outside. He lived to tell the story of the magic call of the piper.

For many years afterward he used to say:

"I am very sad and lonely since all my little playmates went away that day with the piper and I was left alone."

The mayor offered both gold and silver, if only the piper would bring the children back to Hamelin. But it was too late. They never returned to their fathers and mothers. They had gone forever.

From the day the Pied Piper charmed the boys and girls of Hamelin by his wonderful music, and disappeared with them in the mountain side, all time was reckoned in the town. That was in July, 1284.

The people had the story written on the church window, that every one should know how their little ones were taken away.

THE EMPEROR'S SLEEP

Like Barbarossa, who sits in the cave,
Taciturn, somber, sedate and grave,
Till his beard has grown through the table of stone!
~Longfellow— *The Golden Legend*

Many hundred years ago there was a powerful emperor of Germany called Frederick Barbarossa (Redbeard), on account of his long, red beard. When this emperor died, his enemies, who feared him, rejoiced; but his subjects, who loved him, grieved.

As the Britons used to say of their noble King Arthur, so the Germans said of their noble Emperor Frederick Barbarossa:

"He will come again; he is not dead, but awaiting the time when we shall need him."

The emperor, at the head of a hundred and fifty thousand men, lost his life when on his way to the Holy Land. After a long march they came to a famous river. Some people say that part of the vast army crossed the bridge that spanned the stream.

But the emperor, being impatient to join his son, who led the advance-guard, plunged into the water, with his warhorse and heavy armor. The swift current overpowered the aged monarch, and bore him swiftly away.

Others say that Frederick Barbarossa, being wearied with the long march, bathed in the river to renew his strength.

The water was as cold as ice. A sudden chill struck the feeble emperor, and he died on the bank of the famous stream.

Although the emperor died, and his palace beside the river Rhine was destroyed, it is said he lives still, and his servants are heaping up treasures and weapons in his castle, which

> With the rust of centuries still looks down
> On the broad, drowsy land below.

Once a peasant who wandered into a cave in the hills declared he caught a glimpse of the majestic figure of the sleeping emperor. He was sitting, he said, in front of a table of stone, on which he leaned, and over which his long beard flowed.

As the peasant passed, the emperor raised his head and asked:

"What age of the world is this?"

When he heard the peasant's answer, he cried sadly, "Not yet," and settled himself again for another long sleep.

Once in a hundred years he wakens, and calls to his attendant:

> O dwarf, go up this hour
> And see if still the ravens
> Are flying round the tower;
> And if the ancient ravens
> Still wheel above me here,
> Then must I sleep enchanted
> For many a hundred year.
> ~Rückert (Taylor's Tr.)

When the dwarf returns and tells the emperor that the ravens are still flying around the tower, his master sighs and settles himself for another sleep of a hundred years.

When the ravens fly no more around the ruins of the castle, and the emperor's long beard has grown around the table of stone three times, then the trumpet will sound, and Frederick Barbarossa shall come again.

THE LORELEI

On yonder height there sitteth
   A maiden wondrous fair,
Her golden jewels sparkle;
   She combs her golden hair;
With comb of gold she combs it
   And sings, so plaintively,
A strain of wondrous beauty,
   A potent melody.
            ~Heine (Selcher's Tr.)

You have sung this song very often, no doubt, and have seen the picture of the maiden sitting on the rock, high above the water. The old stories tell us that Lorelei was a maiden of wondrous beauty, who lived in the river Rhine. All day she would hide in the river so that no one could see her; but when night came she would climb to a high rock where she could be seen in the moonlight by all who passed by on the river. There she would sit and sing, and comb her beautiful golden hair.

This curious maiden had a wonderful power over all who listened to her sweet singing. The boatmen and fishermen were so enchanted by her wondrous songs that they forgot to guide their boats, which drifted about, and were finally dashed to pieces on the rocks. So many were lost, while listening to her song, that a band of soldiers was sent to carry her off in the darkness. When the soldiers neared the rock where the Lorelei sat singing her sad, sweet melodies, they, too, were spellbound, and could not move.

While the men stood there, held by her magic spell, the Lorelei took off her sparkling jewels and threw them into the river, which began to rise. When the water had reached the top of the great rock, where she was standing, she jumped into a green chariot drawn by horses with white manes, and vanished from the sight of the wondering soldiers who had come to seize her.

The water flowed back where it had been; the magic spell was broken; the river Rhine flowed on peacefully as before.

Another story is that of all the suitors the Lorelei had, there was one knight whom she loved best. He wanted to go to the war to win honor and glory for her sake. She begged him not to go; but he was determined to do so. A long time passed. No word came from the knight, and the maiden was very unhappy. The people declared she had caused so many to be lost in the river by her wondrous singing, that they brought her before the magistrate. She flung herself at his feet and begged to die, for she loved only the knight who had gone away.

The magistrate listened to her story, and bade two knights take her to a convent where she would never be troubled more.

They crossed the river, and drew near a huge rock, which the Lorelei asked leave to climb and take a last look at her home.

The knights consented. As she reached the top of the rock, a boat came in sight. In it stood a knight, clad in complete armor.

At once the maiden saw it was the knight who had gone to war, and whom she mourned as dead.

With joy, she called to the knight, as he stood in his boat far below her. He heard her wondrous voice calling to him, and paid no heed to his boat, which was carried swiftly away by the strong current of the river.

> In tiny skiff, the boatman
>   Is seized with a wild, wild woe.
> He gazeth on high unceasing;
>   He heeds not the cliffs below.
> I fear me the skiff and the boatman
>   Will both „neath the waters drown,
> And this, with her wondrous singing,
>   The Loreley has done.
>   ~Heine (Selcher's Tr.)

The unhappy maiden, seeing the poor knight's danger, leaned forward to save him. In doing so, she fell from the rock that has borne the name of the Lorelei ever since.

Thus perished both knight and maiden in the swift-flowing river.

INDEX OF PROPER NAMES

Al'torf - A town in Switzerland
Andvari - (and'va-rē); King of the dwarfs. **Ar'thur** - King of the ancient Britons
Atri - (a'trē); A town in Italy.
Av'a-lon - The Island of the Blessed, where King Arthur was taken-generally supposed to be Glastonbury
Babieca - (bab-i-ē'ca); "Booby", or the horse of the Cid
Bal'der - God of peace and light
Barbarossa - (bar-ba-ros'a); "Red-beard", also the surname of Frederick I of Germany
Bedivere - (Sir) (bed'i-vēr); a knight of the Round Table
Belé - (bē-lā'); the father of Ingeborg
Bjorn - (byern); a friend of Frithiof
Bri'an Boru - (bo-ro'); "Brian of the Tribute"; an early king of Ireland
Brunhild - (bron'hild); a valkyr, or warrior-maiden
Car-deñ'a - Burial-place of the Cid
Charlemagne - (char'lē-mān); King of France and Emperor of the West
Cid - (sid); "Champion"; also the favorite hero of Spain
Clontarf - (klon-tarf); Brian Boru's last battle with the Danes
Don Fer-nan'do - A cavalier of the court of Portugal
Durandal - (du-ran(g)-dal); the sword of Roland
Ector - (Sir) (ek'tor); the foster-father of King Arthur
Eg'lan-tine - The king's daughter who was punished for her pride
El-li'da - The dragon-ship of Frithiof

Excalibur - (eks-kal'i-ber); the sword which the Lady of the Lake gave to King Arthur.
Fafnir - (faf'nēr); the dragon that was slain by Sigurd.
Fe'lix - The monk to whom a hundred years seemed as one day
Frey - (frī); the god of sunshine in Northern mythology
Frithiof - (frēt'yof); "Peacemaker"; the hero of an old Norse story
Ga'ne-lon - A traitor in the army of Charlemagne
Gessler - (ges'ler); a ruler of the Swiss
Greyfell - (grā'fel); the horse of Sigurd
Guinevere - (gwin'e-vēr); the wife of King Arthur
Hamelin - (ham'e-lin); A town in Germany
Hec'tor - The hero that was slain by Achilles
Hel'gé - A brother of Ingeborg
Hil'ding - The foster-father of Frithiof
Hiordis - (hyor'dis); the mother of Sigurd
Hoenir - (hē'nir); the god of brightness
Hood, Rob'in - The bold outlaw of Sherwood Forest
In'ge-borg - The heroine of an old Norse story who became the wife of Frithiof
Kay (Sir) - (kī); the foster-brother of King Arthur
Kennedy (ken'e-di), King - The leader of the powerful Clan of Gas, and father of Brian Boru
Kin-kō'ra - Palace of Brian Boru
Kirk'ley Hall - The place where Robin Hood died
Le-o'de-gran - Father of Queen Guinevere
Limerick - (lim'e-rik); County in Ireland
Loki - (lō'kē); the god of fire and strife

Lorelei - (lō're-lī); A siren of the river Rhine, after whom a rock in that river was named

Mahon - (ma-hōn'); the brother of Brian Boru

Mal'a-gis - A dwarf in the court of Charlemagne

Mar-i-an - "Maid Marian," who became the wife of Robin Hood

Mar-sil'i-us - The Moorish king to whom Ganelon betrayed Roland

Mer'lin - The enchanter

Mō'dred (Sir) - A nephew of King Arthur, by whom the king was fatally wounded in battle

Mon-ō'nia - Munster in Ireland

O'din - The chief of all the gods in Norse mythology

Ol'i-ver - One of the twelve peers of Charlemagne, and the friend and companion of Roland

Regin - (rā'gin); the teacher of Sigurd

Rich'ard I - King of England, called Coeur de Lion (ker de lē-on'), the Lion-hearted, on account of his bravery.

Rob'ert - King of Sic'i-ly

Rodrigo Diaz - (rōd-rē-gō dē-ath'); the real name of the Cid

Ro'land - A peer and nephew of Charlemagne Sigmund - (sig'mond); the father of Sigurd Sigurd - (zē'gord); the hero of the Volsung family

St. Brand'an - A mysterious island, named for St. Brandan by the natives of the Canary Islands

St. Denis - (sent den'is/French, san-de-nē'); the patron saint of France

Tell, William - The famous hero of Switzerland Thor - The god of thunder

Thors'ten - The father of Frithiof

Tintagel - (tin-ta'jel); a castle on the coast of Cornwall, said to be the birthplace of King Arthur

Tizona - (tē-thō'na); the sword of the Cid

U'thur - The father of King Arthur, known from his rank as Uther Pendragon

Vol'sung - A powerful family of the North, of which Sigurd was the chief hero

Vulcan - (vul'kan); the god of fire, forging, and smelting

Xi-mē'na - The wife of the Cid

www.ingramcontent.com/pod-product-compliance
Lightning Source LLC
Chambersburg PA
CBHW030303100526
44590CB00012B/503